Voices Of Repentance

Lenten Midweek
Vespers

Donald H. Neidigk

CSS Publishing Company, Inc., Lima, Ohio

VOICES OF REPENTANCE

Copyright © 2006 by
CSS Publishing Company, Inc.
Lima, Ohio

All rights reserved. The worship bulletins may be copied for use as intended. No other part of this publication may be reproduced in any manner whatsoever without the prior permission of the publisher, except in the case of brief quotations embodied in critical articles and reviews. Inquiries should be addressed to: Permissions, CSS Publishing Company, Inc., 517 South Main Street, Lima, Ohio 45804.

Scripture quotations are from the Holy Bible, New International Version. Copyright 1973, 1978, 1984 International Bible Society. Used by permission of Zondervan Bible Publishers. All rights reserved.

For more information about CSS Publishing Company resources, visit our website at www.csspub.com or email us at custserv@csspub.com or call (800) 241-4056.

Cover design by Chris Patton
ISBN 0-7880-2395-0   PRINTED IN U.S.A.

*This book is dedicated
to the people of
Calvary Lutheran Church*

Table Of Contents

Introduction	7
Ash Wednesday	
Worship Bulletin	9
Children's Sermon	13
Sermon — The Voice Of The Baptizer	15
Lent Week 1	
Worship Bulletin	21
Children's Sermon	24
Sermon — The Voice Of A Pharisee	26
Lent Week 2	
Worship Bulletin	31
Children's Sermon	34
Sermon — The Voice Of A Sadducee	36
Lent Week 3	
Worship Bulletin	43
Children's Sermon	47
Sermon — The Voice Of A Well-dressed Man	49
Lent Week 4	
Worship Bulletin	55
Children's Sermon	58
Sermon — The Voice Of A Well-fed Woman	60
Lent Week 5	
Worship Bulletin	65
Children's Sermon	68
Sermon — The Voice Of A Tax Collector	70

Maundy Thursday
    Worship Bulletin   77
    Children's Sermon   82
    Sermon — The Voice Of A Soldier   84

Good Friday
    Tenebrae Service — What Wondrous Love Is This?   91
    Scripture And Readings For Good Friday   97

Introduction

Many years ago, after I had concluded the Sunday afternoon service in the Luna County jail in Deming, New Mexico, two prisoners each indicated a desire to acknowledge Jesus Christ as their Savior. I rejoiced to kneel with them in prayer on the concrete floor of their cell. One poured out his heart to the Lord, tears streaming from his face. The other barely spoke a word, never bothering even to close his eyes during the prayer.

A few weeks later I followed up on both of them, inviting them to church where they could grow in their new found faith. The one who made the greatest outward show of prayer and emotion would have nothing to do with me. But the other, the one who showed no emotion whatsoever and who had difficulty offering the simplest prayer, was delighted to see me. Hardly a Sunday had passed before he was in church.

It was perhaps ten years later, when I was serving a church in Kansas, that this second young man wrote me a letter. In it he told me of his continuing faith and active service in his church. Clearly, he was the prisoner who had truly repented. The other had not, despite his impressive display of sorrow for sin.

John the Baptist preached repentance. Those who heard his word — not only with their ears but with their hearts — left the baptismal waters of the Jordan as changed people. That is what repentance is. To repent is to change one's mind and direction. It is to turn away from ungodliness to godliness. It is to move from unfaith to faith in Jesus Christ. It is, as John the Baptist preached, to bring forth fruit corresponding to one's profession of faith.

In this Lenten midweek series, *Voices Of Repentance*, the stories of those who came to John for baptism are told. Their stories reflect the lives of everyday people, though the characters themselves, except for John, are fictional. Suggested by the gospel accounts, the characters include John the Baptist, a Pharisee, a Sadducee, a well-dressed man, a well-fed woman, a tax collector, and a soldier. Hopefully, the worshiper can find a bit of himself in all of these characters. Most importantly, may each worshiper experience true repentance and a growing faith in Christ as the Lenten season unfolds.

Author's Note: Although these are not marked, it is my belief that invocations, prayers, and benedictions in the name of the Holy Trinity should include the sign of the cross before the name of Christ. It is entirely up to the pastor/worship leader to decide whether or not to use the sign of the cross.

Pastor Donald Neidigk

Ash Wednesday

Worship Bulletin

Silent Procession Of The Cross

We Enter God's Presence
Hymn   "On Jordan's Bank The Baptist's Cry"

Invocation
P: In the name of the Father and of the Son and of the Holy Spirit.
C: **Amen.**

The Psalm   Psalm 103:1, 6-12
P: Praise the Lord, O my soul; all my inmost being, praise his holy name.
C: **The Lord works righteousness and justice for all the oppressed.**
P: He made known his ways to Moses, his deeds to the people of Israel:
C: **The Lord is compassionate and gracious, slow to anger, abounding in love. He will not always accuse, nor will he harbor his anger forever;**
P: He does not treat us as our sins deserve or repay us according to our iniquities.
C: **For as high as the heavens are above the earth, so great is his love for those who fear him;**
P: As far as the east is from the west, so far has he removed our transgressions from us,
All: **Praise the Lord, O my soul; all my inmost being, praise his holy name.**

Hymn   "Speak, O Lord, Your Servant Listens"

Confession And Absolution
(The imposition of ashes is incorporated or not incorporated, according to local practices, following confession and just prior to absolution.)

We Hear God's Word

The First Lesson   Isaiah 40:3-8
"Make straight in the wilderness a highway for our God."
L: This is the Word of the Lord.
C: **The Word of our God stands forever.**

The Holy Gospel   Mark 1:1-11
"He will baptize you with the Holy Spirit."
P: This is the gospel of the Lord. What is its fruit of repentance?
C: **Its fruit of repentance for me is to prepare the way for the Lord by acknowledging my sin.**

Children's Sermon

Hymn   "O Living Bread From Heaven"

Sermon   "The Voice Of The Baptizer"

We Respond To God's Word In Faith

Nicene Creed
    I believe in one God, the Father Almighty, maker of heaven and earth and of all things visible and invisible.
    And in one Lord Jesus Christ, the only-begotten Son of God, begotten of His Father before all worlds, God of God, Light of Light, very God of very God, begotten, not made, being of one substance with the Father, by whom all things were made; who for us men and for our salvation came down from heaven and was incarnate by the Holy Spirit of the virgin Mary and was made man; and was crucified also for us under Pontius Pilate. He suffered and was buried. And the third day He rose again according to the Scriptures and ascended into heaven

and sits at the right hand of the Father. And He will come again with glory to judge both the living and the dead, whose kingdom will have no end.

And I believe in the Holy Spirit, the Lord and giver of life, who proceeds from the Father and the Son, who with the Father and the Son together is worshiped and glorified, who spoke by the prophets.

And I believe in one holy Christian and apostolic Church, I acknowledge one Baptism for the remission of sins, and I look for the resurrection of the dead and the life of the world to come. Amen.

Offering

Offering Voluntary "O Dearest Jesus, What Law Have You Broken?"

Prayer Of The Day
P: Eternal God, your Word reminds us that we are grass that withers and flowers that fall. By your Spirit, incline our hearts to heed John the Baptist's call to repentance. Move us to embrace through faith, the one John directed us to, Jesus, the Lamb of God, who takes away the sins of the world. And thus, through our baptism enable us to bring forth abundant fruits of good works. In Jesus' name we pray.
C: **Amen.**

Pastoral Prayers

Response
P: Let us pray to the Lord.
C: **Lord have mercy.**

Lord's Prayer
Our Father who art in heaven, hallowed be thy name, thy kingdom come, thy will be done on earth as it is in heaven.

Give us this day our daily bread; and forgive us our trespasses as we forgive those who trespass against us; and lead us not into temptation, but deliver us from evil.
For thine is the kingdom and the power and the glory forever and ever. Amen.

We Receive The Holy Sacrament
(Order Of Holy Communion follows local practice)

Distribution Hymns   "All Who Believe And Are Baptized"
"Chief Of Sinners Though I Be"

We Depart With God's Blessing
Benediction
P: The voice of one calling in the wilderness,
C: **Prepare the way for the Lord.**
P: The Almighty and Merciful Lord, the Father, the Son, and the Holy Spirit, bless and preserve you.
All: **Amen.**

Closing Hymn   "O God, My Faithful God"

Silent Recession Of The Cross

Ash Wednesday

Children's Sermon

And this was his message, "After me will come one more powerful than I, the thongs of whose sandals I am not worthy to stoop down and untie. I baptize you with water, but he will baptize you with the Holy Spirit." — Mark 1:7-8

Items Needed: a pair of sandals

Welcome, children! It's good to see you here for this Ash Wednesday service. Ash Wednesday is the first day of Lent. Lent is a time we think about what it means to be a holy child of God for whom Jesus died. Sometimes people put ashes on their foreheads as a way of saying they are sorry for their sins and to remind themselves that they need Jesus' forgiveness.

This Lenten season we are thinking about what it means to repent. When we repent we admit we have sinned and we turn away from our sins. But we don't just turn away from our sins. We also turn to Jesus in faith. John the Baptist's job was to call everyone to turn away from their sins, to be baptized and to believe in Jesus.

John the Baptist was a very good man. Jesus even said no one who has ever been born is greater than John. But even as great and good as John the Baptist was, he said of himself that he was not even worthy to untie Jesus' sandals. I brought my sandals to show you. *(show children the sandals)* I only wear them in the summer. When I wear them they get sweaty and smelly and covered with dust. Would you like to untie my stinky sandals and carry them? *(let them answer)* Why not? Yes, because they're dirty and smelly. No one but me will touch them.

But John the Baptist said he wasn't even worthy to do such a lowly job for Jesus. By that, he was telling everyone that Jesus was the most holy and most important person in the whole world, and John was just the lowest servant of Jesus. That's how a repentant Christian feels about himself and Jesus. That's how we feel, isn't it? Jesus is good and holy, and we are lowly and sinful. But the amazing thing is that Jesus loves us and considers us so important he came to die for us. He came to die for you and me to take away all our sins and make us holy! That makes us so happy and thankful we want to serve Jesus and do all he asks. We especially want to tell others about his love. Let's thank Jesus for his love, shall we?

Prayer

Jesus, no matter how hard I try, I can't be as holy as I should be. I'm like John the Baptist, unworthy to untie your sandals, but you love me anyway. You came to forgive me and make me holy by living and dying in my place. Thank you, that by faith you make me worthy to be your servant. In your name I pray. Amen.

Ash Wednesday   **Isaiah 40:3-8**
                                                                              Mark 1:1-11

Sermon

The Voice Of The Baptizer

So, you want to hear about me, John the Baptist, do you? Actually, I'd much rather point you to Jesus. My life only has importance in relation to him. But if knowing more about me will help you hear better what I proclaim about him, then I suppose I could say a few things about myself. You must forgive me, though. I do feel very awkward about this, and I tell you these things very reluctantly. My parents, Zechariah and Elizabeth, the prophets Isaiah and Malachi, these are really whom you should turn to if you would learn more of me.

But as you wish. As with all people, I was in the gracious plan of God long before I was born. You see, all of history is proceeding toward a great end, the day of the Lord when Christ comes in power and glory to judge the world, purifying it with fire and bringing about the restoration of all things to the goodness God intended at first.

As that day approaches, you have a part to play in God's plan. Your part is to repent of sin, to acknowledge God's love and forgiveness that is yours in Christ, and to bring forth the fruits of faith in your life. In addition to that, my part is to prepare the way for Christ by calling you to repent, to be baptized, to live a life transformed by faith.

My calling was made known centuries ago through the prophets. Then as now, the people of God were often rebellious and unbelieving. Idolatry, materialism, the pursuit of pleasure, cruelty to the helpless, trusting in man rather than God; all these described Israel in years past. Through the prophets, God pleaded with his people to return to him and his ways that their lives would be long and happy in the land he had given them, but they refused. At long last, God had no choice but to humble them in their pride. Foreign soldiers destroyed Israel's cities and farms. Many were killed. The survivors were taken away to far-off lands.

In Babylon, they reflected on their sins, and cried out to God for help and mercy. He heard. He always does. Through Isaiah, he promised one who would prepare the way for the Lord who would come to lead his people home. "A voice of one calling: 'In the desert prepare the way for the Lord; make straight in the wilderness a highway for our God. Every valley shall be raised up, every mountain and hill made low; the rough ground shall become level, the rugged places a plain. And the glory of the Lord will be revealed, and all mankind will see it' " (Isaiah 40:3-5).

In a limited way, those words were fulfilled when many of the Jews were allowed to return home after the Persians conquered the Babylonians. But a greater fulfillment remained. All mankind had yet to see the glory of the Lord. So my job is to proclaim the complete fulfillment of that promise in Jesus, the one who is the very glory of God, who came once as a servant and sacrificial lamb, but who comes again as king of all creation.

Though some of God's people returned to Israel, and many were humbled and brought to faith by their experience in Babylon, others quickly forgot and were just as faithless as their ancestors. The prophet Malachi had harsh words for the empty religious ritual of those who returned, whose lives showed how little they valued God's Word and goodness to them. They were offering blind and diseased animals as sacrifices. Worship was thought a burden. Lying and deceit characterized their relationship with neighbors. Divorce was rampant. Few bothered to give God the whole tithe they had promised him.

But soon, the days of their half-hearted love and service to God would be over. A day of accountability was coming. Through Malachi, the Lord warned, "See, I will send my messenger who will prepare the way before me. Then suddenly the Lord you are seeking will come to his temple ... But who can endure the day of his coming? Who can stand when he appears? For he will be like a refiner's fire ... It will burn like a furnace. All the arrogant and every evildoer will be stubble, and that day that is coming will set them on fire ... see, I will send you the prophet Elijah, before that great and dreadful day of the Lord comes" (Malachi 3:1a, 2a; 4:1, 5).

Jesus has said of me that I am that promised coming of Elijah. Literally, of course, I am not Elijah, but in that my job is like his, calling people to repentance and faith, I am Elijah. That is partly why I dress and live as I do. Elijah and other prophets of God dressed in rough leather and hair clothing to set them apart from the worldliness they condemned. Fine clothing and fancy food don't convey a message that this world and its pleasures are passing away. But a life of simple tastes, a life of self-denial does. Thus, I dress as I do and eat what most despise, locusts and wild honey. Why accumulate wealth when all is destined for destruction by fire? This is what you are to remember when you stare at me and are tempted to laugh.

So here I am, a wild-looking man with a humorless message. But I have not always been this way. My childhood and youth were perhaps much like yours. In childhood, I wasn't reared in the poverty I later chose as an adult. We were as well off as anyone. Zechariah, my father, was a respected priest. He was serving in the temple when he learned from the angel that I would be born. My mother, Elizabeth, was an honored lady in the community. How the relatives and neighbors rejoiced when they learned I was born to childless parents!

Being born to an elderly couple had its advantages. I was an only child upon whom was lavished all the attention proud parents can give. I was well educated. As any Hebrew child, I learned to read and write in the synagogue. From my father I was trained in all the learning of the Levitical priesthood. Growing up I would sometimes visit my cousins with whom I played, including Jesus who was but six months younger than I. Though the hand of God was on both of us, our respective callings didn't preoccupy us as small boys. We played tag as any children, we made mud pies, we floated little boats in puddles after the spring rains.

It was when I became a young man that my thoughts turned to God's plan for me. As with countless men of God in every century, I left home and entered upon a life of contemplation, of study, of seclusion. Often, I had conversations with religious leaders; the powerful Sadducees who controlled the priesthood, the Pharisees who were the self-appointed guardians of the Law and public morality, and those who had fled this world for the isolation and self-denial of the desert, the Essenes.

There was something true and yet false about all of them. The Sadducees saw to it that worship was conducted according to the ancient rituals, that all was done properly, as was only right, yet many of them didn't even believe in a spiritual world. They were more than eager to compromise truth in order to maintain their political position.

Pharisees, on the other hand, were utterly committed to obeying the Law of God, every letter of it, including all the traditional interpretations. They tolerated not the slighted deviation from what they considered lawful. But though outwardly obedient and pious, they had no real love for God or neighbor. Some would tithe the smallest bit of spice, but would let their parents starve.

The Essenes who lived apart in the desert in the community of Qumran rejected all this hypocrisy. They sought to live lives of purest devotion to God, baptizing themselves frequently for spiritual cleansing, meditating on the scriptures, preparing for the coming day of the Lord. But how can one love God and neighbor in isolation? God does not call us to prepare for the coming of his Son by *leaving* the world but by living holy lives of faith and compassion *in* the world.

Yes, I live in the desert, I live simply, but I am no recluse. The kingdom of God that I proclaim is not a protected ritual, it is not a legalistic regimen, it is not the solitary life. It is a relationship with God demonstrated in one's relationship with others. It begins with faith and repentance and baptism. It is lived out each day as one bears the fruit of the Spirit; love, joy, peace, patience, kindness, goodness, faithfulness, gentleness and self-control (Galatians 5:22-23).

And it is also something impossible for us to achieve on our own. We need a Savior. And it is the Savior whose way I have been sent to prepare. I think you probably already know a relationship with God and a worthy life in his kingdom are things out of reach, at least by our own efforts. We've all tried and failed. That's why you and so many others have come out to the desert to find me and hear my message, isn't it?

You've tried on your own to please God and you couldn't do it. Your particular sin may not be exactly the same as those addressed by Isaiah; you haven't literally made an idol and worshiped it. Your sin may not be one of those railed against by Malachi; it never occurred to you to bring a one-eyed sacrifice to God's house. Your sin may not be precisely the sin of those coming to me in the desert for baptism. You've never extorted money, and you're not a dishonest tax collector.

Your sins are different. Mine are different. Perhaps your sin is gossip, or disrespect of parents, or some sexual sin. Perhaps it's being uncharitable, or speaking unkindly. Only you know what it is that in your own strength you've been unable to free yourself of. But that's why God sent me, John the Baptist. He's sent me not only to call you to repentance, to call you to change your mind about sin and walk in a new direction, but to point you to one who comes to forgive you and cleanse you from your sins. That one is Jesus, proclaimed to be God's Son by the voice from heaven on the day I baptized him. That one is Jesus whom I proclaim to you today as the "Lamb of God who takes away the sin of the world." Let me make that more specific. That one is Jesus, the Lamb of God sacrificed for *you*, to take away *your* sin.

My message, I know, is full of the threats of God's Law. "... Flee from the coming wrath." "The ax is already at the root of the trees, and every tree that does not produce good fruit will be cut down and thrown into the fire" (Matthew 3:7b, 10). Yes, they are frightening words, and they are intended to frighten. But there is more to my message than fear. Mine is also a message of sweet gospel, of sweet good news. Even my name should tell you that. It is after all, "John," meaning, "God is gracious."

And that is what every repentant sinner, every baptized believer in Jesus finds God to be, gracious, more than willing to forgive and accept you. Repent! Believe in Jesus! Receive the forgiveness God brings you in baptism. And then through his Spirit, bring forth the fruit of faith for him.

You've come a long way into the desert to find me. Your feet are tired and sore. It will be a journey you'll always remember. But may it not be just a memory of a visit to a strange man in strange clothes who ate strange food. May it be the beginning of a new life with a new direction. May you come as a sinner to the river of God's grace. And may you go forth as God's basket overflowing with his fruit.

Prayer
Father in heaven, through your Word proclaimed by faithful John the Baptist, you call us to repentance. Help us trust in the Savior he directs us to, that we might have forgiveness and be ready for the day of his coming. And Lord, through your Spirit may our lives overflow with fruit that benefits others. In Jesus' name we pray. Amen.

Lent Week 1

Worship Bulletin

Silent Procession Of The Cross

We Enter God's Presence
Hymn   "Come To Calvary's Holy Mountain"

Invocation
P: In the name of the Father and of the Son and of the Holy Spirit.
C: **Amen.**

The Psalm   Psalm 51:14-18
P: O Lord, open my lips, and my mouth will declare your praise.
C: **Save me from my bloodguilt, O God, the God who saves me, and my tongue will sing of your righteousness.**
P: You do not delight in sacrifice, or I would bring it; you do not take pleasure in burnt offerings.
C: **The sacrifices of God are a broken spirit; a broken and contrite heart, O God, you will not despise.**
P: In your good pleasure make Zion prosper; build up the walls of Jerusalem.
All: **O Lord, open my lips, and my mouth will declare your praise.**

We Hear God's Word
The First Lesson   Isaiah 29:13-16
"Their hearts are far from me."
L: This is the Word of the Lord.
C: **O Lord, turn our hearts to you.**

The Holy Gospel   John 1:6-9, 15-17, 19-29
"Pharisees who have been sent questioned him."
P: This is the gospel of the Lord. What is its fruit of repentance?
C: **Its fruit of repentance for me is to make straight God's way in my heart.**

Children's Sermon

Hymn "Today Your Mercy Calls Us"

Sermon "The Voice Of A Pharisee"

We Respond To God's Word In Faith
The Apostles' Creed
   I believe in God the Father Almighty, maker of heaven and earth.
   And in Jesus Christ, his only Son, our Lord, who was conceived by the Holy Spirit, born of the virgin Mary, suffered under Pontius Pilate, was crucified, died and was buried. He descended into hell. The third day he rose again from the dead. He ascended into heaven, and sits at the right hand of God the Father Almighty. From thence he will come to judge the living and the dead.
   I believe in the Holy Spirit, the holy Christian church, the communion of saints, the forgiveness of sins, the resurrection of the body, and the life everlasting. Amen.

Offering

Offering Voluntary "Praise The One Who Breaks The Darkness"

Prayer Of The Day
P: Let us pray to the Lord.
All: Holy God, the prophet Isaiah rightly accuses me of honoring you with my lips but not my heart. Deliver me from worship and service based on rules taught by men rather than the leading of your Spirit in the Word. Fill me with the new life that is mine in baptism that I might bring forth fruits of repentance grounded in love. In Jesus' name I pray. Amen.

Pastoral Prayers

Response
P: Lord, in your mercy,
C: Hear us, O Lord.

Lord's Prayer
    Our Father who art in heaven, hallowed be thy name, thy kingdom come, thy will be done on earth as it is in heaven.
    Give us this day our daily bread; and forgive us our trespasses as we forgive those who trespass against us; and lead us not into temptation, but deliver us from evil.
    For thine is the kingdom and the power and the glory forever and ever. Amen.

We Depart With God's Blessing

Benediction
P: The law was given through Moses,
C: Grace and truth came through Jesus Christ.
P: The Almighty and Merciful Lord, the Father, the Son, and the Holy Spirit, bless and preserve you.
All: Amen.

Closing Hymn   "Oh, That The Lord Would Guide My Ways"

Silent Recession Of The Cross

Lent Week 1

Children's Sermon

Woe to you Pharisees, because you give God a tenth of your mint, rue and all other kinds of garden herbs, but you neglect justice and the love of God. You should have practiced the latter without leaving the former undone. — Luke 11:42

Items Needed: a container of spice and a can of food

Hi, children! Welcome to God's house and the children's message. In our services we're learning about John the Baptist and people who came to him for baptism. When people were baptized, John expected them to live differently than they had lived before. Some of the people whom John baptized were Pharisees. Do you know who the Pharisees were? *(give one or two an opportunity to answer)* Pharisees were very religious Jews who tried to obey God perfectly. They knew every commandment and law in the Bible and all the explanations of those commandments and laws, too. Pharisees would never disobey a Law of God if they could help it. They hoped God would give them eternal life by being good. But they were not really as good as they thought they were.

Jesus pointed out to the Pharisees that in obeying God's Laws down to the tiniest detail, they overlooked more important things. I brought some things to show you what I mean. This is a can of spice and this is a can of food. *(show the children)* Pharisees knew God's Word taught them to tithe everything they earned or grew. So, if a Pharisee grew some spice, he would give a tenth of it to God. But if someone were hungry, a Pharisee wouldn't necessarily give the hungry person some food. Some would tithe, Jesus said, but not help their needy parents. What do you think God says about that? *(let children answer)*

Right, it's far more important to care for the needy than to tithe a little bit of spice. That's how a truly repentant person thinks. When we are baptized and believe in Jesus as our Savior, we become very concerned about loving our neighbor and helping him.

Yes, we should always obey God's Law, but loving our neighbor from our heart is the fruit of repentance the Holy Spirit makes grow in our lives, and that's what's really important.

Prayer

Dear God, help me love you and my neighbor from my heart. Show me the needs of others that I can meet. Thank you that Jesus died for my sins. In his name I pray. Amen.

Lent Week 1 Isaiah 29:13-16
John 1:6-9, 15-17, 19-29
Luke 11:42

Sermon

The Voice Of A Pharisee

I am Hasid, a Pharisee. I know that for many, the word "Pharisee" has become a term of scorn and derision. You would look far and wide to find someone who would think it an honor to be called a Pharisee. But I am such a person. Perhaps if you knew more about my sect you would not be so quick to judge.

As you read the story of Christ you will find that Pharisees were not only counted among his enemies, but also among his best friends. Perhaps you remember Nicodemus who buried Jesus, and Saint Paul who became his greatest champion, both of them Pharisees. Not only so, but many of the doctrines held firmly by Christians were taught and defended by Pharisees; doctrines such as divine providence, angels, a day of judgment, resurrection of the righteous to eternal life, and eternal punishment for the wicked.

My origins go back to the time the exiles in Babylon returned to Jerusalem. For many years the remnant of Israel had languished as prisoners and slaves in that far-off land, paying God's just penalty for their sins. For, you see, despite the many prophets who pleaded with them to turn from sin and idolatry, to turn back to God and his holy Law, they had refused. After centuries of their disobedience, God's patience at last ended. Great empires destroyed Israel and Judah, and the people were deported. In Babylon they repented, they pleaded with God to forgive them, to restore them to their land. Many grew old and died as they waited for God to answer. At last he heard. Under Ezra and Nehemiah the people were allowed to go home and rebuild. You would have thought that after paying such a terrible price for their disobedience they would have remembered God and his Law, but they quickly forgot. Once back home, they began to abuse and cheat the poor.

They married the unbelievers who had settled in the land they had left empty. Their worship became empty ritual. Their offerings were half-hearted and incomplete.

But Ezra and other leaders saw the danger of this. He and his allies, the scribes, opposed the compromises and the unfaithfulness. My forebears used whatever methods it took to bring the people back to their senses; words of rebuke, shame, striking the lawbreakers, forced divorces from unbelievers, even banishment. Our very survival as the people of God was at stake. We had to take those measures. After all, what is more important than faith and obedience?

After our return to the land, priests and scribes worked together to restore the people to faith. It was a partnership that lasted a long time. But eventually the priests, who held their jobs by birthright, became more concerned about position and rank than the holiness that befits God's people. More and more, the scribes became the experts in the law, calling both people and priests to submission. Thus, two parties developed among us, the Sadducees who served the temple and worked hand in hand with the rulers to preserve their power, and we Pharisees, "the separated ones," who cared little about who was in power as long as God's worship was kept pure and his Law followed.

Huge changes took place within two centuries of our return to the land. The Persians, who had let us go home, were defeated by Alexander the Great and his armies. Greek language and culture were brought to our country. Many of our people were enamored by anything that was Greek. Even the priests were infected with this cancer that threatened our identity and survival. After Alexander's death, his generals and their descendants ruled the empire. Judah was part of the province of Syria. Antiochus Epiphanes, the Greek king who ruled us, determined to remove all traces of our culture, our language, even our religion, Hellenizing us, turning us all into Greeks.

The worship of pagan gods was reintroduced. Circumcision was prohibited. Jewish athletes competed naked in public games. The temple was desecrated with idols. Only one old man, Mattathias, a priest, a descendant of Hasmon, stood up against this blasphemy. When a Jew was about to offer sacrifice to an idol, Mattathias took a sword and killed him.

Thus began the revolt led by a son of Mattathias, Judas Maccabaeus, "Judas the Hammer," as he was called. It was my ancestors who supported his drive to push out the Greeks, restoring our culture and religion, cleansing the temple and bringing back the worship of God, and the teaching of his Law. We Pharisees were happy to serve as allies of the Maccabees, or more properly the Hasmonaeans, as long as they remained faithful to the one true God and his Law, but when they became more interested in retaining power and establishing a dynasty, when politics replaced adherence to the Law, we opposed them. We refused to compromise our faith, a faith that had cost us so much to establish and maintain.

Eventually our cause won the day. The Hasmonaean Queen Alexandra sided with us. With her influence, Pharisaism became the dominant religious force in Palestine. From her day on, even under the Romans, and regardless of who served as high priest, we Pharisees were acknowledged as the interpreters and protectors of the faith. That's quite an accomplishment when you realize we relied only on the Word of God and not the sword, and there were never more than 6,000 of us.

We had suffered greatly to maintain what we believed to be the true religion. We had lived under the foreign oppressors God had placed over us as penalty for our sins. We had worked tirelessly to establish a system of synagogues to teach the Law of God so that the people might follow it. With all we had gone through to protect the true religion perhaps you can understand why many of us were understandably suspicious, and even hostile, when John the Baptist appeared preaching a baptism of repentance for the forgiveness of sins, something he'd not been given approval from us to do.

Hence, I was not quick to accept John's preaching and submit to his baptism. If it violated the Law of God, I would have nothing to do with it, and I would oppose him to the death. Thus, I and others questioned him about who he was and the authority by which he conducted his ministry. But his answers were all according to the scriptures. I believed him when he said he came in fulfillment of Isaiah's prophecy, "I am the voice of one calling in the desert, 'Make straight the way for the Lord.' " His preaching spoke to my heart as he labeled my companions and me a "brood of vipers." We were like snakes, he said, fleeing the coming fire of God. "Bring forth fruit in keeping with repentance," he commanded as he poured water over me. And then he pointed me to another he had just baptized, Jesus of Galilee. Of Jesus he said, "Look, the Lamb of God who takes away the sins of the world."

Understanding did not come instantly or completely. It took months of reflection on the words of John and of being in that great crowd that followed Jesus before I came to grasp something of what John meant. You see, as a Pharisee, I strove ceaselessly to obey every word of the law, and get others to do the same. But though the Law of God utterly consumed me, I learned I had missed its chief point. I discovered I had been content merely to obey it outwardly and to get others to do the same. If I appeared holy, then I must be holy, I thought. It never occurred to me that real obedience to the law was something that came from within. The Law called me to love God and neighbor from the heart. As my heart was filled with God's love, then it would overflow with loving actions for others.

But as I looked at my heart in the light of God's Law, I found that it was empty of love. Instead it was full of every kind of sin. I had never committed adultery and would have gladly stoned anyone who did, but in my heart I found lustful and adulterous thoughts. I had never raised my hand to kill another, but in my heart I had murdered my brother with hateful feelings.

At first, I wondered how I could bring forth fruits of repentance when I honestly believed I had not done wrong. But when I saw my heart for what it truly was, I knew there was much that needed changing. I was indeed, "a whitewashed tomb" as Jesus later described me, "full of bones" and devoid of any real life from the Spirit.

That is when I began to comprehend John's identification of Jesus as the "Lamb of God who takes away the sins of the world." I was a sinner who needed a sacrificial lamb to take my sins away. I couldn't do it myself. God knows I tried. My whole sect had tried. I had devoted my whole life to becoming a righteous person and had failed. If ever I were to be truly righteous, God would have to make me so.

Then it happened, at the cross. I was there in the crowd, standing off in the distance, hearing the groans of Jesus with every blow of the hammer as the nails were driven into his flesh. I had once heard Jesus say, "I have come to seek and to save that which was lost, and to give my life a ransom for many." Now it made sense. Though outwardly righteous, I was lost, but here was Jesus giving his life for me. His death and resurrection changed me. From a whitewashed tomb I became a blood-washed saint. From being dead in my heart, I became alive in the Spirit. Now fruits of the Spirit nurtured by God's love are replacing works of the law I once performed in my own effort.

My name, Hasid, means "godliness." It's a fitting name because there is nothing I have sought more than to be a truly godly person, but it wasn't until I met John and the person he pointed me to, Jesus, that I truly became one. Now I realize I am godly, but it has nothing to do with all my efforts or the noble heritage of my ancestors. It is God's gift to all who trust his Son. As you repent and turn to Jesus, the Lamb of God, it is your gift, too.

Prayer

Dearest Lord, we confess that all of us have at times been Pharisees. There is none of us who have not looked at ourselves in comparison to others and said, "I am righteous." Forgive us for our pride. Show us that your Law justifies no one, but condemns us all. Then, Lord, direct our hearts to Jesus that we might trust in him and find forgiveness and the gift of righteousness. In his name we pray. Amen.

Lent Week 2

Worship Bulletin

Silent Procession Of The Cross

We Enter God's Presence
Hymn   "In The Cross Of Christ I Glory" (vv. 1-2)

Invocation
P: In the name of the Father and of the Son and of the Holy Spirit.
C: **Amen.**

The Psalm   Psalm 100
P: Shout for joy to the Lord, all the earth.
C: **Worship the Lord with gladness; come before him with joyful songs.**
P: Know that the Lord is God. It is he who made us, and we are his; we are his people, the sheep of his pasture.
C: **Enter his gates with thanksgiving and his courts with praise; give thanks to him and praise his name.**
P: For the Lord is good and his love endures forever; his faithfulness continues through all generations.
All: **Shout for joy to the Lord, all the earth.**

Hymn   "In The Cross Of Christ I Glory" (vv. 3-4)

We Hear God's Word
The First Lesson   Deuteronomy 10:12-22
"Do not be stiff-necked any longer."
L: This is the Word of the Lord.
C: **He is our God, our praise who has performed awesome wonders.**

The Holy Gospel   Matthew 3:4-12
"Sadducees [were] coming to where he was baptizing."
P: This is the gospel of the Lord. What is its fruit of repentance?
C: **Its fruit of repentance for me is to follow not just the letter of God's Law, but its spirit.**

Children's Sermon

Hymn   "The Savior Calls"

Sermon   "The Voice Of A Sadducee"

We Respond To God's Word In Faith

The Apostles' Creed
   I believe in God the Father Almighty, maker of heaven and earth.
   And in Jesus Christ, his only Son, our Lord, who was conceived by the Holy Spirit, born of the virgin Mary, suffered under Pontius Pilate, was crucified, died and was buried. He descended into hell. The third day he rose again from the dead. He ascended into heaven, and sits at the right hand of God the Father Almighty. From thence he will come to judge the living and the dead.
   I believe in the Holy Spirit, the holy Christian church, the communion of saints, the forgiveness of sins, the resurrection of the body, and the life everlasting. Amen.

Offering

Offering Voluntary   "Go My Children With My Blessing"

Prayer Of The Day
P: Awesome and mighty God,
All: **You are the Creator of heaven and earth. As one baptized into your holy triune name, take away my stiff-neck and proud spirit. Enable me to show forth fruits of repentance with acts or kindness toward the fatherless, the**

foreigner, the widow, the hungry, and the hated, showing the world that you are indeed a loving God. In the name of Jesus I pray. Amen.

Pastoral Prayers

Response
P: Lord, in your mercy,
C: **Hear us, O Lord.**

Lord's Prayer
Our Father who art in heaven, hallowed be thy name, thy kingdom come, thy will be done on earth as it is in heaven.

Give us this day our daily bread; and forgive us our trespasses as we forgive those who trespass against us; and lead us not into temptation, but deliver us from evil.

For thine is the kingdom and the power and the glory forever and ever. Amen.

We Depart With God's Blessing

Benediction
P: Flee from the coming wrath!
C: **Produce fruit in keeping with repentance.**
P: The Almighty and Merciful Lord, the Father, the Son, and the Holy Spirit, bless and preserve you.
All: **Amen.**

Closing Hymn "Lord, Dismiss Us"

Silent Recession Of The Cross

Lent Week 2

Children's Sermon

> *... Christ was sacrificed once to take away the sins of many people; and he will appear a second time, not to bear sin, but to bring salvation to those who are waiting for him.* — Hebrews 9:28

Items Needed: a large carving knife and a cross

Welcome back, children! This is the second full week of Lent. During these weeks, we're learning about repentance from John the Baptist and what he told those who came to him for baptism. Repentance is turning from our sins, believing in Jesus, and doing things God's way.

One of the people who came to John for baptism was a Sadducee, a ruler of the people who was also a priest. Sadducees didn't believe in eternal life and resurrection. That's why they're "sad you see." That's just a little joke. As priests, Sadducees would sacrifice animals in the temple as God's Law told them to do. Maybe they used a knife like this one. *(show the knife but don't let children hold it)* To kill an animal, they would cut its throat so its blood would flow out. They believed this turned God's anger away from them.

They were doing what God said to do, but in the New Testament, we are told that animal blood can never take away our sins. Animals were sacrificed to remind us of our sins and show us we deserved to pay for them with our own blood. But God loves us too much to let that happen. That's why he sent Jesus. Jesus' death on the cross is the sacrifice that pays for all our sins so we can be forgiven and not die but have eternal life.

I brought a cross *(let children see it)* to show us how Jesus died. He was nailed to it. When he bled and died there, all our sins were paid for forever. No more sacrifices of animals or anything else needs to be made. I'm surely glad about that, aren't you? All we do is say "Thank you," to God for the gift of his Son. Let's say thank you to God right now.

Prayer

Dear Heavenly Father, thank you for the sacrifice of Jesus for my sins. Because of him I am forgiven and have a home in heaven. In Jesus' name I pray. Amen.

Lent Week 2   **Deuteronomy 10:12-22**
Hebrews 9:28; 10:4
Matthew 3:4-12

Sermon

The Voice Of A Sadducee

Of all the people who came to John for a baptism of repentance, perhaps I am the least likely. I am, after all, a priest, and as a priest, I am thought by most to be closer to God than anyone. I even thought so myself until I heard John's preaching and met Jesus. I am Zadok, a priest and a Sadducee.

Like the Pharisees, we Sadducees have a long and noble heritage, even longer and nobler than the Pharisees. We've never really liked each other. You might say we merely tolerated each other. Ours is a relationship of mutual dependency and barely concealed disdain. They need us. We need them. Without the Pharisees, through whom everything must be approved, we Sadducees would not hold the high priesthood. If they don't like someone, that person doesn't get appointed, or perhaps that person gets removed.

Pharisees control every aspect of the religious life of the people. We, the rightful religious leaders, chafe at this arrangement, but we accept it. After all, it has given us the position and influence we need with the Romans to become the wealthy and aristocratic party that we are. But, we are not mere leeches. It is our reasoned voice and close relationship with the Romans that has so far kept their armies from totally destroying our country and temple. Without us there'd be no Pharisees, no law, no nothing. The Pharisees know this and so they tolerate us. Without us there'd be no one to protect the temple, and if there were no temple, how could God's Law be kept, a Law that requires the daily sacrifices and offerings we priests make before his altar? The Pharisees don't like our privileged caste and our rather secular beliefs, but if they are to obey the Law they claim to cherish, they have to put up with us. As I say, it is an unpleasant but necessary relationship, or at least I once thought it was necessary. Now I realize that Christ is the only sacrifice that really matters and that through him, all of God's people are priests, not just people like me, Zadok.

I have claimed that the heritage of the Sadducees is longer and nobler than that of the Pharisees. That's because only one born into the priestly tribe of Levi, the tribe of Moses, can be a Sadducee. By divine right we inherit our place and role among God's people. No Pharisee can make that claim. While the Pharisees may aspire to be the followers of Moses, we are his blood relatives. We are the descendants of Aaron, the brother of Moses. As priests we looked after the souls of Israel and were stewards of the Law of God for a thousand years before there was even one Pharisee. Perhaps you can understand our resentment.

Now, to be perfectly honest, not every descendant of Levi and Moses is a Sadducee. John who baptized me was the son of a priest, but neither he nor his father Zechariah were Sadducees. You see one only needs to be a Sadducee if he wishes to become rich and powerful, something John had no interest in. As a Levite, John was my relative and no Pharisee. It is perhaps for those two reasons I was drawn to him. At least it made worthwhile a trip into the desert to hear him.

Reluctantly, I must admit that our movement as a sect within Judaism has only been in existence about as long as the Pharisees. Our origins go back to the time of the Maccabees, the priestly family that purged Greek influence from our land and religion. At first, we priests cooperated with the scribes and students of the law who sought to restore the true worship of God. But more and more they sought to impose portions of the scriptures and traditions that we felt were less valuable. We held that the Torah alone, the first five books of Moses, were to be obeyed. Other books were good reading, but didn't have the same weight.

But it is from just such books, the prophets and the writings, that the Pharisees developed their doctrine, along with the commentaries compiled by the rabbis. It is in these books that the Pharisees find their distinctive beliefs about a spiritual world of angels, of predestination, of the bondage of the human will, of divine judgment at the end of the ages, of resurrection to eternal life or damnation.

Sadducees have considered all this to be myth and speculation and contrary to the Torah. Angels are simply appearances of God. Human will is utterly free to determine its own destiny. Surely God is far too busy to plan every detail of our lives. Sadducees think that talk of an afterlife is foolishness. After all, who has ever returned from the dead proving anything else? Death means annihilation of body and soul. To be "gathered unto the fathers" is merely to join them in the grave, not in some paradise called "heaven."

I must say, that is how I once believed, but no longer. You must understand that coming to John for baptism and living a penitent life did not mean I suddenly knew and understood all the implications. When John baptized Jesus and announced him to be, "the Lamb of God who takes away the sin of the world," I really had no idea what he meant. Perhaps he was declaring Jesus to be the rightful high priest and a rival to Caiaphas. By all I could see and hear, Jesus was certainly a more worthy candidate for the office. Caiaphas never once was concerned with anyone but himself, with his position and power, but Jesus was different. While Caiaphas flattered Roman occupiers and sought favors, Jesus was out among the people, preaching good news.

This good news was that in himself, God's kingdom had come. Again and again, he demonstrated it was so. People sick with all sorts of diseases were healed by his word and loving touch, even lepers. No Pharisee or Sadducee would have touched them. The demon possessed and epileptics were freed. Jesus refused no one who came to him; tax collectors, prostitutes, Roman soldiers. If they needed healing, he healed. If they needed forgiveness, he forgave.

And his teaching made far more sense to me than that of the Pharisees. They believed it wrong to pay taxes to Rome. No true Israelite and Messiah would support giving money to the very Gentile dogs who oppressed God's people, they thought. Sadducees, on the other hand, though hating the tax as much as anyone, knew the Romans would get it out of us one way or another. If we didn't pay up, they'd loot Jerusalem and the temple and take our people away as slaves. So we paid and encouraged the people to pay as well. What else could we do?

Once the Pharisees and supporters of Herod came to Jesus and asked him, "What is your opinion, is it right to pay taxes to Caesar or not?" They were hoping both to trap Jesus and embarrass us. If Jesus said, "Pay your taxes to Rome," the people would reject him as the political Messiah they thought him to be. If he said, "Don't pay your taxes," the Romans would arrest him and probably kill him as an enemy of the state. Either way, the Pharisees would be rid of him. But do you know how Jesus answered? He took a coin with the likeness of Caesar on it and said, "Give to Caesar what is Caesar's and to God what is God's." It was masterful! In such simple words he showed that there are really two kingdoms, one of this world and another of God. Jesus is king of God's world, a world that wants the hearts of men, not their coins. I couldn't help but laugh at this resounding defeat for the Pharisees.

Then it was our turn to be humiliated. As I've already said, we Sadducees rejected any concept of an afterlife. We also differed with the Pharisees in how we understood marriage law. According to Moses, if a man died without giving his wife a child, the man's brother had to marry her and hopefully give her a child on behalf of the dead man. In the Sadducee's view, this could only be done if the first marriage hadn't been consummated, in other words if it were only an engagement and not a real marriage. Otherwise, it would be incest. The Pharisees, on the other hand, believed the law applied regardless of whether the marriage had been consummated.

Hoping to discredit both Jesus and the Pharisees, as well as make believers in resurrection look foolish, a Sadducee told a story and concluded it with a question. "Teacher," he said, "Moses told us that if a man dies without having children, his brother must marry the widow and have children for him. Now there were seven brothers among us. The first one married and died, and since he had no children, he left his wife to his brother. The same thing happened to the second and third brother, right on down to the seventh. Finally, the woman died. Now then, at the resurrection, whose wife will she be...?" They really thought they'd gotten Jesus with this one, as well as the Pharisees. But Jesus amazed us all, and convinced even me. "You are in error," he said, "because you do not know the scriptures."

Imagine telling the Pharisees they didn't know the scriptures! "At the resurrection people will neither marry nor be given in marriage; they will be like the angels in heaven," said Jesus. That comment was aimed at us who didn't believe in angels. Then Jesus went on, and this clinched it for me. "But about the resurrection of the dead — have you not read what God said to you, 'I am the God of Abraham, the God of Isaac, and the God of Jacob'? He is not the God of the dead but of the living."

Do you get it? Do you understand? Jesus is quoting from the Torah, the only book we Sadducees really believe! Why did I never notice this before? If Abraham, Isaac, and Jacob were all dead, and not just dead but annihilated, God would have said, "I *was* the God of Abraham, the God of Isaac, and the God of Jacob." But that's not what he said. He said, "I *am* their God!" That means they are alive today thousands of years after their deaths, enjoying life in God's presence.

I'd heard John say Jesus was the Lamb of God and thought it had something to do with the priesthood, but I misunderstood. Jesus was no mere replacement for Caiaphas, the high priest. No, Caiaphas was in the same league as a tax paid to Caesar, a worldly token, like a coin, compared to the high priesthood of Jesus. Caiaphas, as high priest, was content merely to see that a supply of lambs was furnished to the temple for the sacrifices. As such he was little more than a butcher. But Jesus is a high priest who gives himself as the lamb. That's what John meant when he called Jesus "the Lamb of God who takes away the sin of the world."

It all came together for me on the day Jesus was crucified. As he hung there suffering unimaginable agony, he prayed for Pharisee, Sadducee, Roman, for all of us. He prayed, "Father, forgive them for they do not know what they are doing." Then he spoke once more of eternal life, saying to the believing thief crucified beside him, "Today you will be with me in paradise." Soon after that he prayed his last prayer, "Father, into your hands I commit my spirit," and then he died.

Next, the unimaginable happened, an earthquake! There was hardly any damage, except to the curtain in the temple, the curtain concealing the Most Holy Place. It was ripped right down the middle! Anyone could look right in there and see the place of God's presence. What could it mean? It meant my service as a priest wasn't needed anymore, that's what it meant! No longer would any other priest or I be required to offer daily sacrifice. The only blood that mattered had now been shed, the blood of Jesus. Through the blood of Jesus, the true Lamb of God, every believer is welcome in God's presence.

Life has changed so much for me since John's baptism and the day I followed Jesus. After his resurrection, I began to sense his Spirit in my life. Privilege and money don't mean to me what they once did. I've discovered nothing's more fun than giving away what I don't need to someone else who does need it. Once death was truly my enemy; it depressed me. It doesn't anymore. Sometimes I'm afraid as I think of it, but not as I once was, not since I learned that Abraham, Isaac, Jacob, the thief, all of them, are all very much alive and waiting to welcome me into heaven's joy. And Jesus is there with them, arms wide, ready to embrace me, but not just me, you also.

Prayer

Living Savior, you came to give your life that we might have life. Help us find joy in the forgiveness of our sins and the certain hope of eternity with you in paradise. In Jesus' name we pray. Amen.

Lent Week 3

Worship Bulletin

Silent Procession Of The Cross

We Enter God's Presence
Hymn "Open Now Thy Gates" (vv. 1-3)

Invocation
P: In the name of the Father and of the Son and of the Holy Spirit.
C: **Amen.**

The Psalm Psalm 91:1-6, 9-10, 14-16
P: He who dwells in the shelter of the Most High will rest in the shadow of the Almighty.
C: **I will say of the Lord, "He is my refuge and my fortress, my God, in whom I trust."**
P: Surely he will save you from the fowler's snare and from the deadly pestilence.
C: **He will cover you with his feathers, and under his wings you will find refuge; his faithfulness will be your shield and rampart.**
P: You will not fear the terror of night, nor the arrow that flies by day,
C: **Nor the pestilence that stalks in the darkness, nor the plague that destroys at midday.**
P: If you make the Most High your dwelling — even the Lord, who is my refuge —
C: **Then no harm will befall you, no disaster will come near your tent.**
P: "Because he loves me," says the Lord, "I will rescue him; I will protect him, for he acknowledges my name.
C: **He will call upon me, and I will answer him; I will be with him in trouble, I will deliver him and honor him.**
P: With long life will I satisfy him and show him my salvation."

All: He who dwells in the shelter of the Most High will rest in the shadow of the Almighty.

Hymn "Open Now Thy Gates" (vv. 4-5)

We Hear God's Word

The First Lesson Isaiah 58:1-9a
"When you see the naked ... clothe him."
L: This is the Word of the Lord.
C: Shout it aloud, do not hold back.

The Holy Gospel Luke 3:1-11
"The man with two tunics should share."
P: This is the gospel of the Lord. What is its fruit of repentance?
C: Its fruit of repentance for me is to follow not just the letter of God's Law, but its spirit.

Children's Sermon

Hymn "Drawn To The Cross"

Sermon "The Voice Of A Well-dressed Man"

We Respond To God's Word In Faith

The Apostles' Creed

I believe in God the Father Almighty, maker of heaven and earth.

And in Jesus Christ, his only Son, our Lord, who was conceived by the Holy Spirit, born of the virgin Mary, suffered under Pontius Pilate, was crucified, died and was buried. He descended into hell. The third day he rose again from the dead. He ascended into heaven, and sits at the right hand of God the Father Almighty. From thence he will come to judge the living and the dead.

I believe in the Holy Spirit, the holy Christian church, the communion of saints, the forgiveness of sins, the resurrection of the body, and the life everlasting. Amen.

Offering

Offering Voluntary "Take My Life"

Prayer Of The Day
P: Let us pray ...
All: God of mercy and justice, I humbly acknowledge that my words of faith are often contradicted by my actions. I ask for your presence and blessing in worship while quarreling with my neighbors and ignoring the needs of others. As your baptized child, forgive my sins, work true repentance in my heart, and move me to store less and give more to help those who have little. In the name of Jesus I pray. Amen.

Pastoral Prayers

Response
P: Lord, in your mercy,
C: Hear us, O Lord.

Lord's Prayer
Our Father who art in heaven, hallowed be thy name, thy kingdom come, thy will be done on earth as it is in heaven.
Give us this day our daily bread; and forgive us our trespasses as we forgive those who trespass against us; and lead us not into temptation, but deliver us from evil.
For thine is the kingdom and the power and the glory forever and ever. Amen.

We Depart With God's Blessing
Benediction
P: Every valley shall be filled in, every mountain and hill made low.
C: The crooked roads shall become straight, the rough ways smooth. And all humankind will see God's salvation.

P: What should we do then?
C: **The Almighty and Merciful Lord, the Father, the Son, and the Holy Spirit, bless and preserve you.**
All: Amen.

Closing Hymn "On What Has Now Been Sown"

Silent Recession Of The Cross

Lent Week 3

Children's Sermon

... for all of you who were baptized into Christ have clothed yourselves with Christ.   — Galatians 3:27

Items Needed: a bag of clothing; shirts, pants, coat, and similar items

Welcome back, boys and girls. We're now in the third week of Lent. It won't be long now until we're celebrating Easter, the day Jesus rose from the dead, giving us all the hope of resurrection. In the Gospel Lesson for today, John the Baptist told the people with extra clothes to share with those who didn't have any. That's how they could show they were really sorry for their sins and wanted to do things God's way.

I brought a bag of clothes from my closet that I never wear. *(show the children a few items)* I was saving them for my sons when they got bigger. But guess what I've discovered? They don't like the style of clothes I do, so they won't wear them. Then I thought, they aren't worn out, so maybe I'll wear them again, but I'm not the same size any more. They don't fit.

What should I do with them? *(children may suggest giving them to a charity such as Goodwill)* Yes, that's a good idea. I could give them away so someone who can't afford new clothes will have something to wear. If I don't give them away soon, they may fade or get moths in them. Then they would be wasted.

Why do you suppose people are sometimes reluctant to give away things they really don't need? *(a child may say, "Because they think they might need them someday.")* Yes, they think they might need them. Or they're afraid they won't get more if they give something away. But God always meets our needs, doesn't he?

As Christians, we believe God meets not only our physical needs but our spiritual needs as well. He clothes us with Jesus in our baptism. That means he covers all our sins with the goodness of Jesus. Do you trust God to save you from your sins and give you a home in heaven? *(let children respond)* Yes, I believe that, too. If we can trust God to give us eternal life we can trust him to give us what we need for this life, too. That means we don't have to keep everything. We can give things away. We can be generous.

Let's pray that God will help us trust him so we can be generous.

Prayer

Dear Father, you give me all I need for this life and the next, help me know that whether I have many things or only a few, I can still be generous. Help me give freely, knowing you will always provide for me. In Jesus' name I pray. Amen.

Lent Week 3　　　　　　　　　　　Isaiah 58:1-9a
　　　　　　　　　　　　　　　　　Galatians 3:27
　　　　　　　　　　　　　　　　　Luke 3:1-11

Sermon

The Voice Of A Well-dressed Man

You may call me Labash. It means, "clothed." I'm the one John the Baptist was speaking of when he said, "The man who has two tunics should share with him who has none." I don't think I could have been more surprised or puzzled when John spoke those words to me. But I had asked what I might do to show my repentance and that's what he told me.

Yes, I have some extra clothes. Who doesn't? But that doesn't mean I'm rich, no, not at all. In fact, I'm a man of very modest means. The tunic Jesus referred to was the *chiton* (kee tone), a common undergarment nearly everyone wears next to his body. It's usually made of cotton and extends to just above the knees, though some go all the way to the ankles. There's a hole for the head and two holes for the arms. Sometimes the *chiton* has sleeves. If you saw one you would think it looked like a nightgown. If one is very poor, this may be the only garment he has. Deprive a poor man of his *chiton* and he would be truly naked. But even the person of the most modest means ordinarily has a change of underwear, wouldn't you agree?

That's why I was puzzled when John told me to give away my other tunic. That would leave me with only one *chiton*, not naked, but without one to wear while washing the other. Most people I know have far more in the way of clothing than just one or two changes of underwear. There's also the outer garment, the *meil* (may eel), worn over the tunic. It's much the same but looser and gathered about the waist with a piece of stout cloth or leather called a girdle. In the folds of the *meil* above the girdle one can carry all sorts of items. It's like a portable shopping cart that keeps one's hands free. Even the girdle can be used as a pouch for carrying small or precious items.

Usually, there's one more garment. That's the cloak or *simlah* (seem la). It is essentially a large decorated blanket of heavy woolen cloth with fringe on the corners. When the weather is cold, the *simlah* is wrapped tightly around the body. On warm days, it is thrown loosely over the shoulder and held in place with the arm, something like a toga. The *simlah* is the most versatile of garments, useful for carrying bundles or serving as a sleeping bag at night or even as a shade from the sun. It's so necessary and valuable that Moses in the Law forbade keeping a poor man's cloak over night as collateral for a loan. He needed it to survive.

By the time of Jesus, creditors had discovered a way around this law. They no longer took the *simlah* as collateral. They had discovered that they might give the poor man his cloak back for the night and then never see it or their money again. So now they take the *chiton* in pledge, and keep it until the poor man pays them back. No one wants to go very long without underwear, they reason. But you don't need it to survive, like the *simlah*. So, they're being compassionate, they think, but they also get their money.

This brings me back to John's words, his telling me that if I have two tunics, two sets of underwear, give one to the poor. I am clothed, *Labash*, as my name says, but that doesn't mean I have all the items I've described. In addition to my tunics, I have only my cloak, my *simlah*. With clothes being so scarce and expensive, I can only afford a tunic for work, and my cloak for cold nights. To give away my one extra tunic, I would be almost naked. That's rather an extreme demand, wouldn't you agree? At least that's how I thought, until I heard Jesus. Then the words of John seemed moderate in comparison.

Shortly after I was baptized, I became a follower of Jesus. It was Jesus for whom John was preparing the way by preaching repentance and baptism for the forgiveness of sins. John had made me more aware of my sins than anyone before, especially with his words about my tunics. He showed me how greedy I was, to keep two tunics for myself when some of my neighbors had nothing. Reluctantly, I gave my extra *chiton*, that precious change of underwear away. But any misgivings I had were replaced with feelings of joy as I watched a near-naked man put it on. His eyes, once filled with shame and embarrassment, immediately began to glow with a new sense of dignity.

There, I'd done it! I'd successfully repented of my sinful greed and born the fruit of repentance John commanded. At least that's what I thought until I heard Jesus. When John directed me to him as the Lamb of God who takes away the sins of the world, I followed him. If John believed in him, so would I. I had traveled all the way to Capernaum from Judea to hear Jesus, but I wasn't alone. Hundreds had come from all over Galilee, the Decapolis, Jerusalem and Judea just to catch a glimpse of him. On the mountain near the Sea of Galilee, he spoke to us. Laws I thought I had kept, I discovered I had broken, like murder and adultery. Even to think hateful or lustful thoughts was the same as breaking the law, Jesus taught. I was glad I had proven myself to be a generous man by giving away my second tunic. At least there was something about myself I could be proud of, I reasoned.

But then Jesus demolished even that shred of self-righteousness. "But I tell you, do not resist an evil person. If someone strikes you on the right cheek, turn to him the other, also." What, allow someone to hit me, twice? "And if someone wants to sue you and take your tunic, let him have your cloak as well." My cloak, my *simlah*? Did Jesus realize the position that would put me in, me who now only had two items of clothing? I didn't have an outer garment, the *keil*, only my underwear and cloak. Did he really expect me to give away both, leaving me naked?

Yes, that's exactly what he expected. He wanted me to realize that real repentance is what happens when I find myself completely and utterly naked, having no hope in myself, with nothing to cling to but God in faith. Every good deed I prided myself in, every extra garment in my closet, every extra jar of food on the shelf, every loose coin in my purse was just one more barrier between me and faith that finds sufficiency in Christ alone. To repent truly and trust in the Lamb of God John pointed me to was to throw away every crutch, not just the extra ones in the closet, but the very ones I relied on to stand up.

Was Jesus using hyperbole, exaggeration? Absolutely! But it's a most necessary exaggeration. The goal of Jesus in these extreme words was to teach his followers total dependence on God for all their needs in every situation; danger, hunger, nakedness, death, whatever it might be. When we have so many things we no longer need to trust God for our daily provision, we have too many things. In that same Sermon on the Mount, Jesus went on to teach us how to pray. He said in words I recite often, "Give us this day our daily bread." Did you notice that Jesus didn't teach us to pray, "Give me today the bread I'll need for the whole week, or next month, or the coming decade?" No! Give me only enough each day that I learn to rely completely on you, God. That's how I am to pray, and that's how I can give away my extra tunic, or anything else I might have. I know God will provide me whatever I need when I need it.

God has richly given us all things to enjoy, and nothing is to be rejected if received with thanksgiving, scripture teaches. It also urges us to follow the example of the ant that labors all summer long so it might have something to eat in the winter. But the same book that teaches us to enjoy God's gifts with thanksgiving and store up what is needed for the winter also exhorts us to work with our hands that we might have something to share. Since all we have comes from God, whether it is plenty or little, we will always have enough to share with someone less fortunate. That's what faith believes.

Jesus taught his disciples about God's provision when he sent them out on their first missionary journey without him. "Do not take along any gold or silver or copper in your belts," he told them. "Take no bag for the journey, or *extra tunic*, or sandals or a staff, for the worker is worth his keep." Imagine going on a long journey with nothing but the clothes on your back! How would you survive? By faith, of course, by a faith that moves you to love God and neighbor with deeds of compassion. I don't know how long the disciples were gone, but when they got back they told stories of the wonders God had worked, and no one complained that he had gone naked or hungry.

Since I gave away that extra tunic, I've marveled again and again at the way God has provided for my needs. My life is much simpler. I once worried constantly about things that might be stolen or lost, or how I would fix something that broke. Now I don't. In the past I would store things away, saving them for a special occasion, which somehow never came. But no matter how carefully I stored things away for safekeeping, they got stolen or lost or broken anyway. The few extra clothes I saved became moth eaten and faded. So now I just give things away while they are still useful to someone in need. And you know, I haven't gone naked yet, even with just one tunic.

Even as God has given me all the clothes I need each day, I've learned his Son, Jesus, gives me all the clothes I need for eternity. When my clothes closet is empty, somehow God gives me what I need for my body. He does the same for my *soul* closet. Once I had a spiritual closet filled with all sorts of garments I thought would impress God; garments such as trying to be a moral person, being born into a religious family, doing good deeds. Believe me, I hung on to every item thinking I would need it to convince God to give me a home in heaven.

Now I know he freely gives me the spiritual clothes I need just as he does the physical. God's Word says, "All of you who were baptized into Christ have clothed yourselves with Christ." That means that as God's baptized child, as one who has followed Jesus in faith, I can empty my old spiritual closet as well. All the righteous clothing I need to enter God's presence is his free gift to me in Jesus. Jesus, himself, is my righteous clothing. In my baptism, by faith, I have put on Jesus and as I do, God no longer sees my sins. He only sees the pure-white garments of his Son.

I bet you have a few more clothes than you need. Do what I did. Give them away. You'll never miss them and they will make someone who needs them very happy. As you clean out that bedroom closet, don't forget to empty the spiritual one, but don't bother giving away all that self-righteous apparel that's hanging there. God doesn't want it, and neither does anyone else. Just throw it out, and let God give you a whole new wardrobe by faith in his Son.

Prayer

Dear God, forgive us for clinging to things we don't need. Help us to trust your daily provision that we freely and generously share all we have, knowing that everything comes from you. Lord, as we clean out our clothes closet, by your grace clean out our spiritual closets, our hearts, and then clothe us with the righteousness of your Son, Jesus. In his name we pray. Amen.

Lent Week 4

Worship Bulletin

Silent Procession Of The Cross

We Enter God's Presence
Hymn "All Who Believe And Are Baptized" (v. 1)

Invocation
P: In the name of the Father and of the Son and of the Holy Spirit.
C: **Amen.**

The Psalm Psalm 146
P: Praise the Lord, Praise the Lord, O my soul.
C: **I will praise the Lord all my life; I will sing praise to my God as long as I live.**
P: Do not put your trust in princes, in mortal men, who cannot save.
C: **When their spirit departs, they return to the ground; on that very day their plans come to nothing.**
P: Blessed is he whose help is the God of Jacob, whose hope is in the Lord his God,
C: **The Maker of heaven and earth, the sea, and everything in them — the Lord, who remains faithful forever.**
P: He upholds the cause of the oppressed and gives food to the hungry. The Lord sets prisoners free,
C: **The Lord gives sight to the blind, the Lord lifts up those who are bowed down, the Lord loves the righteous.**
P: The Lord watches over the alien and sustains the fatherless and the widow, but he frustrates the ways of the wicked.
C: **The Lord reigns forever, your God, O Zion, for all generations.**
All: **Praise the Lord. Praise the Lord, O my soul.**

Hymn "All Who Believe And Are Baptized" (v. 2)

We Hear God's Word

The First Lesson   1 Kings 17:7-15
"There was food every day."
L: This is the Word of the Lord.
C: **The jar of flour was not used up and the jug of oil did not run dry in keeping with the Word of the Lord.**

The Holy Gospel   Luke 3:7-11
"The one who has food should [share]."
P: This is the gospel of the Lord. What is its fruit of repentance?
C: **Its fruit of repentance for me is to share the abundance of my food with the hungry.**

Children's Sermon

Hymn   "My Hope Is Built On Nothing Less"

Sermon   "The Voice Of A Well-fed Woman"

We Respond To God's Word In Faith

The Apostles' Creed

I believe in God the Father Almighty, maker of heaven and earth.

And in Jesus Christ, his only Son, our Lord, who was conceived by the Holy Spirit, born of the virgin Mary, suffered under Pontius Pilate, was crucified, died and was buried. He descended into hell. The third day he rose again from the dead. He ascended into heaven, and sits at the right hand of God the Father Almighty. From thence he will come to judge the living and the dead.

I believe in the Holy Spirit, the holy Christian church, the communion of saints, the forgiveness of sins, the resurrection of the body, and the life everlasting. Amen.

Offering

Offering Voluntary   "Fruitful Trees, The Spirit's Sowing"

Prayer Of The Day
P: Let us pray ...
All: Sovereign Lord, you credit righteousness to all by faith in your Son. Deliver me from resting in my deeds of the past while doing little for the hungry of the present. Give me ears to hear the calling of my baptism to a new life in Christ that is rich in acts of compassion toward others. In the name of Jesus I pray. Amen.

Pastoral Prayers

Response
P: Lord, in your mercy,
C: **Hear us, O Lord.**

Lord's Prayer
Our Father who art in heaven, hallowed be thy name, thy kingdom come, thy will be done on earth as it is in heaven.
Give us this day our daily bread; and forgive us our trespasses as we forgive those who trespass against us; and lead us not into temptation, but deliver us from evil.
For thine is the kingdom and the power and the glory forever and ever. Amen.

We Depart With God's Blessing

Benediction
P: Every tree that does not produce good fruit will be cut down and thrown into the fire.
C: **What should we do then?**
P: The man with two tunics should share with him who has none.
C: **And the one who has food should do the same.**
P: The Almighty and Merciful Lord, the Father, the Son, and the Holy Spirit, bless and preserve you.
All: **Amen.**

Closing Hymn   "Son Of God, Eternal Savior"

Silent Recession Of The Cross

Lent Week 4

Children's Sermon

John answered, "The man with two tunics should share with him who has none, and the one who has food should do the same."
— Luke 3:11

Items Needed: a package of chopped dates and small bags of wheat, barley, and rice

Hello, boys and girls. It's so good to see you again! During Lent this year we're thinking about John's baptism and his call to repentance. Have you all been baptized? *(let children respond)* I'm glad you've been baptized. If you haven't been baptized, I would love to talk with you and your parents about it privately. God has wonderful gifts for us in baptism.

In baptism God also calls us to repent, to change our minds about sin. God wants us to decide that sin is bad so we'll turn away from it and turn to Jesus and do things God's way. Part of doing things God's way is sharing. People with extra clothes share with the poor the clothes they don't wear. People with extra food share some of their food with people who are hungry.

In Bible times, just as in many parts of the world today, most people didn't have very much food, just barely enough to survive. In Asia, people depend on rice to survive. In many other places they depend on wheat or barley. I've brought some samples to show you. *(show the children the samples)* Sometimes the grain is eaten raw, but most people would rather have it cooked and made into cakes or bread.

You and I have much more to eat than just grain. We have all kinds of other vegetables as well as meat and snack food. Those things can be expensive and hard to find in other parts of the world. In some parts of the world a real treat is eating raisins or dates. Would you like to try a date? *(give each child a piece of date)*

We are very fortunate to be blessed with so much food. We have more than enough to share, don't we? God gives us all the food we need for this life and he gives us Jesus so we can have eternal life. God loves us so much! Sharing our food with hungry people is one way we can show God how much we love him. Let's ask God to help us do that.

Prayer

Dear God, thank you for giving me all the food I need for this life. Thank you that through Jesus I have eternal life, too. Help me show your love by sharing my extra food with others. In Jesus' name I pray. Amen.

Lent Week 4   **1 Kings 17:7-15**
Luke 3:7-11 (John 6:35-51)

Sermon

The Voice Of A Well-fed Woman

You can tell from looking at me that I'm no glutton. As most people in my community, I'm rather thin but strong. I am Tamar. You can tell from my name that my parents often thought about food. Tamar means "date palm." But I'm sure they had other reasons for giving me that name. What a lovely tree the date palm is! It grows tall and sways gracefully in the wind. Its lush crown of leaves can be used to build shelters. It lives long, up to two centuries, and each year it produces a crop of delicious fruit. How perfectly that describes the ideal Hebrew daughter, tall and graceful, useful, long-lived, producing lots of fruit, children!

For an ordinary woman like me, finding and preparing food is my chief daily task. Oh, there are other tasks of course, caring for children, spinning thread and making cloth, drawing water at the village well, gathering firewood. But without food and water we soon die, so seeing that my family has food and water is my first responsibility.

My husband, Ezra, is a laborer for King Herod, Tetrarch of Galilee. He works in one of Herod's many olive groves. Ezra is gone by sun up and returns home after sun down. Six days a week he labors, bringing home one denarius, a small silver coin each day. With four children to feed, this is just enough money to buy barley for bread. So I, too, must find food for our family.

Each morning I hurry to the market with my denarius and haggle with the grain sellers, buying from them wheat or barley, whichever is cheapest. Usually it's barley. This I grind with a hand stone into flour for bread. After baking bread, I scour the countryside around our village for edible plants and nuts. Gourds are useful, too. These I dry and make into cups and bowls or dippers and storage containers. Sometimes I'm lucky and find a beehive full of honey. Whatever I find that I don't need that day, I take to the market and sell. This way I can buy extra things such as salt or spices.

Meanwhile, my elderly mother watches the younger children. The older ones work in our garden tending the beans, lentils, cucumbers, and onions that grow there. When there is extra, this too I sell, bringing home a few copper coins that keep us from being among the poorest of the poor. Sometimes when things are going well, and my gourds or honey or cucumbers have gotten me a nice profit, I buy dried fish from the wives of fishermen beside the Sea of Galilee. Meat is too expensive for our family. Only once a year do we have lamb during the Passover celebration, and even then, we join with other families and share the cost.

I said, when things are going well we might have fish; things don't always go well. Once my husband, Ezra, was injured in the olive grove. Another worker smashed Ezra's hand with a mallet by accident as a stake was being driven. It was months before he could work again. In the mean time, I still had my mother and my four children to feed. I was forced to glean in the fields. The children were too young to be of much help in foraging for food, but God was good and somehow we survived.

I don't tell you these things so that you'll feel sorry for me, but so you'll understand that I am neither extremely poor, nor well off. My lot is really not much different than most of my neighbors. Very few of us manage to do much more than survive. Oh, there are a few merchants and bankers who seem to have plenty. The priests do well. We villagers see to that. And the politicians, the hangers-on in Herod's palace, enjoy a soft life, but at the expense of their freedom.

I am by no means wealthy, but my husband is working and we have a home. It's small and sparsely furnished, but it's shelter. We're all clothed and it's not often that we go without food. Even so, very seldom do I have in my house today the food my family will need tomorrow. Yet somehow God has provided for our needs day by day. There always seems to be just enough, but hardly ever too much.

So why would John say to me on that day I came to him for baptism, "Let the person with food share with him who has none"? Shouldn't he have directed those words to the wealthy? The tax collectors coming for baptism had plenty of money, money they'd gotten from overcharging people like my husband. The Sadducees were rich thanks to their political connections. The soldiers had generous portions of food doled out to them daily as part of their wages. Let them give the extra food, I thought at first.

When there were others who had so much more, why should I be asked to share my food, me with seven people to feed? But then I remembered that's exactly what people of faith have always done. And as they've done it, God has always provided for them. Many years ago Elijah, a prophet much like John, asked a poor woman to share her food. Her circumstances were far worse than mine. She was a widow. There was a drought in the land. She had only enough flour and oil to make one last loaf of bread. She planned to share this loaf with her son and then die.

That was her situation when Elijah came to her home asking for a loaf of bread. At first she protested, but Elijah told her not to be afraid. He said to make him the loaf of bread, then make another for herself and her son. God would see to it that she still had enough. A woman of faith, she didn't refuse. She gave Elijah the bread, and just as he'd told her, her jar of flour was not used up and her jug of oil did not run dry until the day the Lord gave rain on the land. She believed. She gave. And she and her son continued to have bread until the drought was broken.

I worship the same God as Elijah, the same God who helped that widow. If she could give Elijah her last loaf of bread and still be provided for, then God could do the same thing for me. John wasn't even asking me to give away my last loaf of bread, and there wasn't any drought and I wasn't a widow. He was just asking me to share what I had with someone who had nothing. I did what John said, and since then I have never gone hungry, though even today I have no idea where I'll find bread tomorrow.

As the years have gone by and as I've followed Jesus whose way John prepared, I've learned there's more to life than bread. There was a time when survival was my chief concern. I would lie down on my mat next to my exhausted husband at night worrying about where I would find food in the morning, especially if I'd had to spend that day's denarius on medicine for a sick child. Then in the morning after I had somehow found food for the day, I worried where I would find food for the night. But then I learned from Jesus that there was more to life than bread made from flour.

It was there by the river that I met Jesus. He had just been baptized. He was the one John said was, "the Lamb of God who takes away the sins of the world." I wanted to follow Jesus that very moment, but he disappeared into the crowd. Later, I learned that he had traveled deep into the desert to pray and fast in preparation for his ministry. For forty days he ate nothing. When his hunger was most intense the devil came and tempted him. "If you are the Son of God," the devil sneered, "tell these stones to become bread."

Jesus could have done it. After all, he was the one through whom God had made everything. If he could make Adam from the ground and Eve from a rib, he could make bread from stones. But Jesus didn't come to entertain the devil or prove things to him. He came to take the place of sinners like me who face temptation every day, and who sometimes fail. Jesus' hunger was real. His temptation was real. But for you and me, he didn't fail. He trusted God to provide for his needs. He said, "It is written, 'Man does not live on bread alone, but on every word that comes from the mouth of God.' " It was a verse from scripture I knew but had forgotten. It reminds me that I am more than a mere body needing bread and water. I am also a child of God who needs the bread of life for my soul. My body will die someday, no matter how well fed it is. But it's only the Word of God that feeds my soul, nourishing it, giving it faith and strength for eternal life, eternal life that begins as I believe the Word, and continues in its fullest sense at the resurrection.

I wasn't at the Last Supper Jesus shared with his disciples, but often I gather with other followers to celebrate it on the Lord's day. It has become the most cherished event in my life. The bread and wine are blessed with the words Jesus spoke, "This is my body," and "This is my blood," given and shed for you for the forgiveness of sins. I don't fully understand the mystery that takes place in those holy moments, but I do know that God is feeding me with the Bread of Life and that I'm partaking of a sacred meal that will never leave me hungry. The bread I bake in my oven leaves me hungry, but not this meal. When I receive the body and blood of Jesus in his supper, I think back to the words he spoke on another occasion. "I am the bread of life," he once said. "I am the living bread that came down from heaven. If anyone eats this bread he will live forever." Some of the Jews who opposed Jesus argued about what he meant by those strange words. He explained, "This bread is my flesh which I will give for the life of the world."

They still didn't understand. I didn't either, really. But now I'm closer to understanding. Yes, my family and I need daily bread to survive, but to live eternally we need the Bread of Life, Jesus. God sent him to die for our sins and give us this life. As we hear God's Word, as we believe in Jesus, as we eat at his table, we receive Jesus and life.

If I can believe in Jesus for eternal life, I can believe in him for daily life, too. The one is a gift of God's grace, so is the other. Life today and life forever all come from God as a gift through his Son. "Give us this day our daily bread," I pray to my Heavenly Father as Jesus taught me. He always does and he always will. The cross of Jesus and his empty tomb are all the proof I need.

Body and soul, I'm cared for. Convinced of that, even an ordinary person of very modest means like me can always give away another loaf of bread, even if it's my last loaf. I don't know where my next loaf is coming from, but I know the one who gives it, and that's enough for me.

Prayer

God, creator, provider, and Savior, you have given us all we need for eternal life in the person of your Son, Jesus. Believing this, help us know that you will also give us all we need for this life as well, and thus fill us with confidence to share our food with others. In Jesus' name we pray. Amen.

Lent Week 5

Worship Bulletin

Silent Procession Of The Cross

                      We Enter God's Presence
Hymn   "O Trinity, O Blessed Light" (vv. 1-2)

Invocation
P: In the name of the Father and of the Son and of the Holy Spirit.
C: **Amen.**

The Psalm   Psalm 145:1, 8-16
P: I will exalt you, my God the King; I will praise your name for ever and ever.
C: **The Lord is gracious and compassionate, slow to anger and rich in love.**
P: The Lord is good to all; he has compassion on all he has made.
C: **All you have made will praise you, O Lord; your saints will extol you.**
P: They will tell of the glory of your kingdom and speak of your might,
C: **So that all men may know of your mighty acts and the glorious splendor of your kingdom.**
P: Your kingdom is an everlasting kingdom, and your dominion endures through all generations. The Lord is faithful to all his promises and loving toward all he has made.
C: **The Lord upholds all those who fall and lifts up all who are bowed down.**
P: The eyes of all look to you, and you give them their food at the proper time.
C: **You open your hand and satisfy the desires of every living thing.**
All: **I will exalt you, my God the King; I will praise your name for ever and ever.**

Hymn "O Trinity, O Blessed Light" (v. 3)

We Hear God's Word

The First Lesson 1 Kings 12:1-15
"Lighten the yoke your father put on us."
L: This is the Word of the Lord.
C: His Word lightens our yoke.

The Holy Gospel Luke 3:7-13
"Don't collect any more than you are required."
P: This is the gospel of the Lord. What is its fruit of repentance?
C: Its fruit of repentance for me is to be generous and compassionate.

Children's Sermon

Hymn "Alas, My God"

Sermon "The Voice Of A Tax Collector"

We Respond To God's Word In Faith

The Apostles' Creed

I believe in God the Father Almighty, maker of heaven and earth.

And in Jesus Christ, his only Son, our Lord, who was conceived by the Holy Spirit, born of the virgin Mary, suffered under Pontius Pilate, was crucified, died and was buried. He descended into hell. The third day he rose again from the dead. He ascended into heaven, and sits at the right hand of God the Father Almighty. From thence he will come to judge the living and the dead.

I believe in the Holy Spirit, the holy Christian church, the communion of saints, the forgiveness of sins, the resurrection of the body, and the life everlasting. Amen.

Offering

Offering Voluntary "There Is A Balm In Gilead"

Prayer Of The Day
P: Let us pray ...
All: God of righteousness, source of all blessings, physical and spiritual, keep me from all dishonesty or theft whether it be great or little. As one who is baptized into Christ, enable me to bring forth in my life fruits of repentance, especially the confidence that you will provide for all my needs in wholesome ways. In the name of Jesus I pray. Amen.

Pastoral Prayers

Response
P: Lord, in your mercy,
C: **Hear us, O Lord.**

Lord's Prayer
Our Father who art in heaven, hallowed be thy name, thy kingdom come, thy will be done on earth as it is in heaven.
Give us this day our daily bread; and forgive us our trespasses as we forgive those who trespass against us; and lead us not into temptation, but deliver us from evil.
For thine is the kingdom and the power and the glory forever and ever. Amen.

We Depart With God's Blessing

Benediction
P: Repent and be baptized every one of you in the name of Jesus Christ for the forgiveness of your sins (Acts 2:38a).
C: **And produce fruit in keeping with repentance.**
P: The Almighty and Merciful Lord, the Father, the Son, and the Holy Spirit, bless and preserve you.
All: **Amen.**

Closing Hymn   "Lord Of Glory, You Have Bought Us"

Silent Recession Of The Cross

Lent Week 5

Children's Sermon

Tax collectors also came to be baptized. "Teacher," they asked, "what should we do?" "Don't collect any more than you are required to," he told them. — Luke 3:12-13

Items needed: a jar or pouch of 100 pennies

Hello, boys and girls. Welcome back! In the Bible there are several groups of people who weren't well liked. Tax collectors were the least liked of all. They were Jews who collected taxes for the Romans. Other Jews thought they were disloyal to God and their country. Tax collectors were often dishonest and cruel.

Taxes were expensive. Let me show you what I mean. Here's a dollar's worth of pennies. *(empty the pouch or jar and show the children)* Is someone here good at math? Great, you can keep track of the money. Let's suppose you worked hard on your farm to earn this money. Now the first tax collector comes by. You give him twenty of these pennies as your tax on the grapes you harvested. Now you give him ten pennies as your tax on your grain harvest. Now you give him five pennies as tax on your land. You owe him another five pennies as head tax, and one more penny as income tax. How much do you have left? *(let the math expert answer)* You have just 59 pennies left.

Now let's go to town and sell our grapes and wheat. We load everything on our donkey cart. When we get to the road we find a tax collector who charges us five pennies for a toll. When we get to the bridge, another tax collector charges us five more pennies. When we get to the town gate, we pay five pennies to the tax collector there to let us through. When we arrive at the market, we pay five more for a place to sell our crops. How many pennies are left? *(math expert answers)* Yes, I think that's 39.

Now we sell our grapes, and pay five pennies in tax on the sale, and another five pennies when we sell the wheat. That leaves us with 29 pennies, right? If we use some of the money we made selling our crops to buy some things we need in town, we have to pay a tax on that, too. On the way home we have to pay the gate tax and the bridge tax and the road tax all over again. How's our math expert doing? *(let expert answer)* You get the idea. Now you understand why no one liked tax collectors. Even the tax collectors felt guilty. That's why some of them came to John for baptism hoping that God would forgive them. And, God did forgive them through Jesus. Jesus is the Lamb of God who takes away the sins of tax collectors and our sins, too.

Prayer

Dear God, thank you that you forgive all who turn from sin and trust in Jesus. Help me to know that by faith in him, I am forgiven. In Jesus' name I pray. Amen.

Lent Week 5   **1 Kings 12:1-15**
                                                                                  Luke 3:7-13

Sermon

The Voice Of A Tax Collector

So you're a sinner thinking about returning to God, coming back to the assembly of his people, doing things his way for a change. Is that it? Good! The time couldn't be better! If you had wanted to do that before Jesus came, I can tell you from experience, it would have been next to impossible. I am Teshubhah (Te-shoe-bah), a tax collector and the son of a tax collector. In fact, all of the men in my family are tax collectors and have been for centuries, ever since the Romans took over Palestine. You see paying taxes to the Romans is viewed by many as a sin against God who alone should be our king. To be the one who collects the taxes is seen as an even worse sin.

When someone becomes a tax collector, no pious practicing Jew will have anything to do with him, or his family. That more or less ensures that one's relatives will be unemployed and destitute unless they become tax collectors, too. It's an unfortunate situation that affects generation after generation, a situation for which there seems to be no escape, except through repentance.

My parents were hoping that I might be the one to break free from the tax-collecting profession. They were hoping I would be the one to repent and be welcomed back into the mainstream of Hebrew society. Thus they gave me my name, Teshubhah, which means "repentance" or "returning." But I was unable to return for the same reasons they were unable.

The rabbis had made repentance virtually impossible for a sinner like me. They had developed a system of repentance that covered every conceivable sin. There was the sin of *breached command*. If at the moment one broke a command of God, he cried out for mercy; he would be forgiven. A sin of *prohibition* required not only repentance, a turning back to God and his law, but sacrifice on the Day of Atonement. *Purposed sin*, which would result in death or being cut off from the people, necessitated both repentance and sacrifice, but also great personal suffering. For *openly profaning the name of God*, only the death penalty would suffice.

Mine was *purposed sin*. For my repentance to be acceptable, I was expected to fast, to publicly acknowledge my sin, and to make restitution. I was required to give up my job and pay back many times what I had wrongly taken from people. As the rabbis might say, if I had wrongly taken just one board from another's house, I was to tear down my house, pay him back, and then become a distributor of alms to the poor. And, having done all this, it was thought that if I truly repented, I would immediately die, death being the evidence of my changed heart. Even then there was no real assurance that God had forgiven me, but at least the rabbis would then think well of me. Do you still wonder why so few of us tax collectors bothered to repent? If there was still no hope for us, we might as well keep doing what we did best, and that was make money.

About 300 years before I came along, the Romans discovered that collecting taxes was more efficiently done when it was contracted out. The Equestrians, the aristocratic knights of Rome, were forbidden to practice the trades or engage in commerce. So to make money, they organized themselves into corporations that bought the tax-collecting privilege from the government. They then hired regional collectors who in turn hired local collectors. At every level, each collector kept a portion of the take until finally the stockholders got their share. Whatever they got above what the government required was profit.

A few years before I got into the business, Caesar had eliminated most of the middlemen except for the local contractor and his employees. I was one of those bottom-rung employees, but it was still a lucrative enterprise. There were two varieties of taxation. One was general taxation. It was collected by the *Gabbai*. General taxes included a head or poll tax on everyone, income tax, and ground tax. Poll tax payment was required until age 65. Ground tax involved payment of taxes on real estate and its produce. A tenth of all grain and a fifth of all wine belonged to the government, as did one percent of one's income. With fixed rates, the *Gabbai* had a comparatively easy job.

Collecting the taxes on commerce and travel was the responsibility of the *Mokhes* of which I was one. We were stationed on every road, at the entrance to every city and village, at markets, at every port or dock where boats loaded or unloaded cargo, at bridges and dams. Goods, pack animals, axles and wheels, even travelers carrying nothing but the clothes on their backs were taxed. If a traveler needed to pay a tax on his donkey but had no money, we would take his donkey and give him an inferior one in change.

Everything was unloaded and searched by the *Mokhes* to determine the amount due, but the assessment was far from objective. If I knew and liked you, you might be charged less, or nothing. If I didn't know or like you, you can imagine the trouble you'd be in. Whatever I decided, that's what you would pay. And pay you would, because I worked for Rome.

Maybe that will help you understand why we tax collectors were so reviled and hated by our fellow Jews. We worked for the enemy, we were rich, and they could do nothing about it, except exclude us from the religious life of the people. And that's what the religious leaders did with a vengeance, making repentance and forgiveness for tax collectors all but impossible.

That's why so many of us flocked to John the Baptist who seemed to offer hope. John didn't turn us away like the rabbis. He offered a baptism of repentance for the forgiveness of our sins, and his conditions of repentance were far more reasonable. "Don't collect any more than you are required," he told us. That was fair. At least I didn't have to tear down my house and become a beggar, as some wanted us to do. But even after baptism and determining to treat each taxpayer with fairness and honesty, I still wasn't accepted by the people. I still wasn't welcome in the synagogue or temple. My neighbors still wouldn't eat with me.

Then I found someone who did welcome me, Jesus, to whom John directed me when I was baptized. Jesus didn't give me an impossible list of requirements to fulfill as the other rabbis did. He didn't tell me to do anything except follow him. And, when the rabbis and Pharisees complained that Jesus had eaten with me, he simply said, "It is not the healthy who need a doctor but the sick. I have not come to call the righteous, but sinners to repentance."

That was me, sick with guilt over my sins, eager to repent but locked out by the synagogue doorkeepers, but not by Jesus. "Follow me," he said, and I did. And what did I find but a great company of people like myself who had found Jesus, or should I say, had been found by Jesus! There were dozens of tax collectors just like me, among them my colleague, Matthew. He'd left his tax booth to become a disciple of Jesus. Others who repented were still collecting taxes, except now they did it with decency and fairness, and they were happy! Regardless of how the religious leaders treated them, they had become compassionate, caring men, often giving away more than they took. Indeed, their compassion and generosity put those pinched-face Pharisees to shame. My friend, Zacchaeus, gave half his possessions to the poor and paid back those he had cheated four times the amount. No Pharisee or rabbi ever did that! We were a happy company that thronged around Jesus, clinging to his robe, straining our ears for every word he spoke, thrilled to be touched by one so holy. Tax collectors, former prostitutes, shepherds, sinners all, and every one of us embraced by the love of God we found in him. He didn't seem to care what others thought of his associating with us. He just answered, "The Son of Man came to seek and to save what was lost."

I was one of those lost people Jesus sought. He sought me with his word of welcome and forgiveness. He saved me when he died on the cross at Calvary. He didn't deserve to die. He'd done nothing wrong except let his goodness outshine the false righteousness of his enemies. It was when he died that I learned what John meant when he said of Jesus, "Behold, the Lamb of God who takes away the sins of the world." All my sins were nailed with Jesus to the cross, all those categories of sin made up by the rabbis, all my inadequate attempts at repentance. "Father, forgive them," Jesus had prayed for his enemies. Then, just before he died, he cried out, "It is finished!" And it was! My sins were gone. At long last I was forgiven and cleansed and accepted by God.

His death has changed me so. Oh, I'm still one of the hated *Mokhes*, but I have a very different approach to my work. I no longer view it as a way to getting rich as I once did, but as a way to bear witness to my Savior. I don't overcharge any more as I once did. And, when I find someone who truly can't pay, I often pay, telling the person, "Even as I am paying your debt, Jesus has paid mine."

When a traveler burdened with a great load comes by, forced yet again to set it down and have it inspected, I help him ease it to the ground. Then I give him a cooling cup of water. When I'm done with my inspection, I help him pack it all up, carry it down to the dock, and load it on the boat. Then I tell him, "Even as I help carry your burden, Jesus has carried my burden of sin, all the way to the cross."

You'll remember that I said the rabbis considered a tax collector truly repentant only if he immediately died after completing all the steps of the repentance ritual. I would suggest that there is greater evidence of repentance. Consider what happened just the other day at my tax booth. A blind man needed to write a letter to be carried by a friend to its destination. He had no money to pay a scribe and the one who would carry it did not know how to write. I overheard the friend say to the blind man, "Let's visit the booth of Teshubhah, the tax collector. He knows how to write. He'll help you."

Except for when I met Jesus and he forgave my sins, that was the greatest moment of my life. At last, two of my own people saw me no longer as their enemy but as their friend. For these two men, 200 years of hostility were forgotten because a tax collector had been changed by Jesus. Indeed, whatever the reason for hostility, whether it is language or culture or race or something else, when the love of Jesus shines through you, it can turn hostility into trust and friendship. Do you have a reputation you can't live down, a history of past actions others won't let you forget? Believe me, when the love of Jesus shines through you brighter than the sins he's carried away, they'll forget.

I better go. This old gentleman coming toward us seems to be having some trouble with his oxen. They're probably just tired and thirsty from their journey. I've got a bucket here with some water. After I've given them a drink there'll be plenty of time to unload the cart and see what the man owes. Why, it's old Joshua! "Hello, Joshua! Have a seat here at my booth while I give those animals some water. Say, how's the family? You know, Joshua, I have a friend who offers you water that will never leave you thirsty. Would you like to hear about him?"

Prayer
Jesus, you turn tax collectors and prostitutes into caring saints by dying for their sins and changing their hearts by faith. Change our hearts, too, Lord. Help us to be known not for our sins, but for your love that shines through us. In your name we pray. Amen.

Maundy Thursday

Worship Bulletin

Silent Procession Of The Cross

We Enter God's Presence
Hymn　　　　　　　　"On Jordan's Bank The Baptist's Cry"

Invocation
P:　In the name of the Father and of the Son and of the Holy Spirit.
C:　**Amen.**

The Psalm　　　　　　　　　　Psalm 140:1-4, 6, 8, 12-13
P:　O Lord, I say to you, "You are my God." Hear, O Lord, my cry for mercy.
C:　**Rescue me, O Lord, from evil men; protect me from men of violence,**
P:　Who devise evil plans in their hearts and stir up war every day.
C:　**They make their tongues as sharp as a serpent's; the poison of vipers is on their lips.**
P:　Keep me, O Lord, from the hands of the wicked; protect me from men of violence who plan to trip my feet.
C:　**Do not grant the wicked their desires, O Lord; do not let their plans succeed, or they will become proud.**
P:　I know that the Lord secures justice for the poor and upholds the cause of the needy.
C:　**Surely the righteous will praise your name and the upright will live before you.**
All:　**O Lord, I say to you, "You are my God." Hear, O Lord, my cry for mercy.**

Hymn　　　　　　　　　　　"Renew Me, O Eternal Light"

Confession And Absolution   Malachi 4:1-2a; Acts 2:38-39;
Psalm 51:3-4, 9; 1 John 1:9; 2:2 (paraphrased)
P: Surely the day is coming; it will burn like a furnace. All the arrogant and every evildoer will be stubble, and that day that is coming will set them on fire, says the Lord Almighty.
C: **But for you who revere [his] name, the sun of righteousness will rise with healing in its wings.**
P: Repent and be baptized for the forgiveness of your sins. And you will receive the gift of the Holy Spirit.
C: **The promise is for [us] and [our] children, and for all who are far off — for all whom the Lord our God will call.**
P: Through his prophets speaking through Holy Scripture, God calls us to confess our sins and to repent of them, turning to Jesus Christ, the Lamb of God, that we might be forgiven.

(silent confession of sin)
P: Merciful God,
C: **I know my transgressions and my sins are always before me. Against you, and you only, have I sinned and done what is evil in your sight, so that you are proved right when you speak and justified when you judge. Hide your face from my sins and blot out all my iniquity. Create in me a pure heart, O God, and renew a steadfast spirit within me.**
P: Our gracious God has heard your cry for mercy. He is faithful and just, and forgives you all your sins through the atoning sacrifice of his Son, Jesus Christ. In the name of the Father and of the Son and of the Holy Spirit.
All: **Amen.**

Collect Of The Day
P: Let us pray ... Lord Jesus Christ, as we recall the day of the institution of your supper, grant that we partake of the mystery of your body in true faith and repentance that we would be moved to accept our place in life with contentment and joyfully serve you and our neighbor. In your name, ever one God with the Father and the Holy Spirit, we pray,
All: **Amen.**

We Hear God's Word

The First Lesson   Amos 5:1, 11-15

"Seek good and not evil."

L: This is the Word of the Lord.
C: **Hate evil, love good, perhaps the Lord God Almighty will have mercy on us.**

The Holy Gospel   Luke 3:7-8a, 14-20

"Don't extort, don't accuse ... be content."

P: This is the Word of the Lord. What is its fruit of repentance?
C: **Its fruit of repentance for me is to be just in my dealings with others, and be content with God's blessings.**

Children's Sermon

Hymn   "I Lay My Sins On Jesus"

Sermon   "The Voice Of A Soldier"

We Respond To God's Word In Faith

Nicene Creed

I believe in one God, the Father Almighty, maker of heaven and earth and of all things visible and invisible.

And in one Lord Jesus Christ, the only-begotten Son of God, begotten of His Father before all worlds, God of God, Light of Light, very God of very God, begotten, not made, being of one substance with the Father, by whom all things were made; who for us men and for our salvation came down from heaven and was incarnate by the Holy Spirit of the virgin Mary and was made man; and was crucified also for us under Pontius Pilate. He suffered and was buried. And the third day He rose again according to the Scriptures and ascended into heaven and sits at the right hand of the Father. And He will come again with glory to judge both the living and the dead, whose kingdom will have no end.

And I believe in the Holy Spirit, the Lord and giver of life, who proceeds from the Father and the Son, who with the Father

and the Son together is worshiped and glorified, who spoke by the prophets.

And I believe in one holy Christian and apostolic Church, I acknowledge one Baptism for the remission of sins, and I look for the resurrection of the dead and the life of the world to come. Amen.

Offering

Offering Voluntary "The Lamb"

Offering Prayer
P: Lord, you look with compassion on the oppressed and call your people to do the same. We confess that often we have not. Instead, we have lavished your material blessings on ourselves and turned a deaf ear to the needy and a blind eye to those who suffer injustice. Forgive us and change us through your word in our baptism. May thankful fruits of repentance overflow in our lives for your glory. May these offerings be acceptable fruits. In Jesus' name we pray.
All: **Amen.**

Pastoral Prayers

Response
P: Lord, in your mercy,
C: **Hear us, O Lord.**

Lord's Prayer
Our Father who art in heaven, hallowed be thy name, thy kingdom come, thy will be done on earth as it is in heaven.

Give us this day our daily bread; and forgive us our trespasses as we forgive those who trespass against us; and lead us not into temptation, but deliver us from evil.

For thine is the kingdom and the power and the glory forever and ever. Amen.

We Receive The Holy Sacrament
(Order Of Holy Communion follows local practice)

Distribution Hymns   "The Gospel Shows"
                                                   "Delay Not, Delay Not"

We Depart With God's Blessing
Benediction
P: He will baptize you with the Holy Spirit and with fire.
C: **His winnowing fork is in his hand to clear his threshing floor and to gather his wheat into his barn. O Lord, make me your wheat.**
P: The Almighty and Merciful Lord, the Father, the Son, and the Holy Spirit, bless and preserve you.
All: Amen.

Closing Hymn   "Go To Dark Gethsemane"

Silent Recession Of The Cross

Maundy Thursday

Children's Sermon

The next day John saw Jesus coming toward him and said, "Look, the Lamb of God, who takes away the sin of the world!"
— John 1:29

Items Needed: heavy weights such as dumbbells

It won't be long now, will it, boys and girls? Easter is this Sunday! What is Easter, anyway? *(let children answer)* Yes, it's the day Jesus rose from the dead. Do you know why Jesus died? *(children may say, "To pay for our sins.")* That's exactly right. Jesus died to take away the burden of the whole world's sins.

This evening we read that soldiers were coming to John for baptism. Their consciences were bothering them. Soldiers often did bad and cruel things. They were carrying a heavy load of guilt from their sins and wanted to be freed from it. Soldiers were also very strong. They could carry 100 pounds up to 24 miles in five hours.

I brought some dumbbells with me. *(let children try lifting them)* People exercise with these to build up their muscles. These weigh just five pounds each. Can you imagine how heavy 100 pounds would be?

Now imagine how heavy our sins must be. We can't put sins on a scale but they surely make our hearts feel weary and burdened like we're carrying a heavy load. That's how the soldiers must have felt. They wanted to get rid of their load of sin. They wanted to be forgiven and change their ways. They wanted to do good things for people.

Where do you suppose that heavy burden of sin went when the soldiers were baptized and forgiven? Maybe you think it went into the water. It didn't really. It was carried by Jesus. When Jesus died on the cross, all the sins of the whole world, the soldiers' sins, your sins and mine, everyone's sins were placed on Jesus. What a heavy burden that was!

I'm so thankful Jesus bore the weight of all our sins, aren't you? Let's thank him.

Prayer

Dear Jesus, thank you for taking the heavy burden of all my sins and dying on the cross to pay for them. Now that I am forgiven, help me do what's right and tell others how they can be forgiven. In your name I pray. Amen.

Maundy Thursday   Amos 5:1, 11-15
John 1:29
Luke 3:7-8a, 14-20

Sermon

The Voice Of A Soldier

What is a soldier in the Roman army doing at a river getting baptized by John? I knew you'd ask. I'm Miles *(Mee-less)*, a soldier in an auxiliary unit attached to one of the legions occupying the Province of Syria of which Jerusalem is a part. Actually, I'm not Roman, I'm German, but I enlisted in the army since that was the only way I thought I could get somewhere in life.

The benefits were part of it. After 25 years of service — if a soldier lives that long — he's granted citizenship with all its privileges, he gets a pension and a farm in Asia, and most importantly, he's finally allowed to marry. According to military law, enlisted men can't marry, at least officially. But unofficially, many of us take common-law wives. Others find the "no marriage" rule a useful excuse for having more than one woman in different parts of the empire, letting them all think they'll be brides some day.

But retirement benefits don't seem all that important when you're twenty years old. If you're hungry and cold and trying to survive in a German forest, warm clothes and food are what you're after. And that's what the army offered me, three meals a day, sturdy warm clothes, and reliable shelter. But it didn't come easy. As a recruit I had to prove myself before final acceptance by the Tribune, and the training was brutal. First, there was physical conditioning, much as a gladiator would endure. We would fight for hours with equipment heavier than the real thing, furiously attacking posts buried in the ground. Then, after learning the basic moves, we'd fight each other with real weapons tipped with wood or leather for safety.

Along with learning to fight, a man had to demonstrate that he could march 24 miles in five hours loaded with all his gear that weighed about 100 pounds. This included armor, a sword, dagger, two javelins, a shovel or mattock, cooking gear, food, warm clothes, and anything else we were told to carry. At the end of the march, we were trained to set up a camp that resembled a fortified Roman town in less than two hours. This meant digging a ditch twelve feet wide and nine feet deep around the entire perimeter, an area large enough to contain six to ten thousand soldiers with all their animals, wagons, siege engines, and pontoon boats. The camp was then bisected with two roads, the commanding general's tent at the center. The various sub units of cohorts, centuries, and cavalry were assigned to the four quadrants of the camp. Each camp was laid out in exactly the same way each time we stopped with every tent, man and officer, and piece of equipment assigned to the same place as in the previous camp. This reduced confusion and promoted efficiency and speed.

The smartest recruits and those with a valuable trade fared the best. These were assigned as bakers, armorers, bookkeepers, or carpenters. Those without such skills were given fatigue duty. That meant digging latrines, caring for animals, cutting stone for roads, and the like. It was grueling work from which unskilled soldiers like me dreamed of escaping.

Occasionally we would engage an enemy, but seldom was there a frontal attack against forces equal to ours. When that happened it was usually one Roman army against another. Most of our fighting was against an unseen enemy that used hit-and-run tactics. Our light infantry and cavalry would go after them and take prisoners for interrogation while the main army would simply occupy and guard the frontier.

The kind of army I've described is hugely expensive. Oh, it brings great benefits wherever it's sent; good roads, public water systems, improved health standards, prosperity to merchants who supply it, but someone has to pay for it, and that's the local population. That's where tax collectors figure in, and that's what brought me to Judea where John baptized me.

I was an occupying soldier, essentially a job filled with boredom. I'd moved up some in the ranks by then, and was no longer assigned to fatigue duty, but I'm not sure my promotion was much of an improvement. My new job was serving as a bodyguard for a tax collector. Someone had to protect these weasels in order to keep the money flowing in and the bills paid, and I was the man.

Why would they need protection? Because they were as brutal and efficient an army as any of the legions of Rome. They were at every road, every gate, every bridge, every dock, and every farm. They were there with their hand out, bleeding the people into poverty. After a while that makes people resentful. They get disrespectful. They get belligerent. In fact, if a tax collector finds himself alone and surrounded by a mob of angry people, he could be in real trouble. He could be beaten, stoned, stabbed, robbed, or whatever the mob feels like doing. So to keep this from happening and to ensure a reliable revenue source, soldiers like me get assigned to tax collectors as personal bodyguards.

That's how I, Miles, the soldier, came to be there with Teshubhah *(Te-shoe-bah)*, the tax collector, the day he decided to venture into the wilderness to hear John preach beside the Jordan River. I already had my religion and wasn't interested in going with him, but I had no choice. To be recognized as a tax collector when surrounded by hundreds of resentful Jews was not a good situation. My job was to protect him, so that's what I did. Little did I know that my being there would lead to my becoming a Christian.

My religion was the worship of Mithras, the Persian sun god. This was the religion of many Roman soldiers. Mithraism taught that the sun god had killed a great bull out of which every living creature on earth arose. All who were initiated into the mysteries of Mithraism through baptism and eating sacred bread were assured of eternal life. Eternal life sounded good, especially to a soldier who never knew when he would die in battle.

But one thing Mithras couldn't offer me was deliverance from guilt that plagued me. As a soldier I had done many of those things we are often charged with. I had killed when I didn't need to, when I could have taken prisoners. I had raped helpless women whose husbands had died in battle or had been taken away as slaves. I had needlessly stolen the valuables of subject people, people such as these Jews. And as guard for this tax collector I had used my power as a soldier to extort money for his benefit and mine.

We had quite a system going. He would tell someone how much was owed. The taxpayer would protest, and often rightfully so. I would "discover" something taxable and charge him with unlawful concealment, even though I was the one who had planted the item. He would deny it, and I would say he was under arrest, whereupon, he was totally at my mercy. After all, I had found the goods. The tax collector was my witness. The offender was going to jail, despite the weeping and pleas of his wife and children. He was going to jail, unless of course he immediately agreed to pay the previously assessed tax and a hefty fine. They almost always agreed and the tax collector and I would split the profits.

And why not? My wages consisted of coarse bread, cheese, cheap wine, and peas. Seldom was I paid in hard cash. They owed it to me, I rationalized, but I knew better. I hadn't been taught the Ten Commandments of the Jews, but I knew what I was doing was wrong. My conscience and heart were heavy, and Mithras wasn't helping me.

Then I heard John. He offered me a solution to my guilt and a way out that was absent from Mithraism. Standing in line beside Teshubhah as I waited for him to be baptized, John began speaking directly to me as though I had come to be baptized, also. At first I was embarrassed and tried to divert his attention to someone else, but John kept looking at me, "You, soldier, you are in danger of the fire of God's wrath! You who have raped and burned and stolen from the innocent, do you think you can escape? Do you think Rome can deliver you from hell? Repent and escape the flames with this tax collector friend of yours!"

"What am I to do?" I asked, surprised at the sound of my own voice actually speaking to this strange-looking man who proclaimed a foreign God.

"Turn from your sins that have enslaved you. Be baptized and receive God's forgiveness," he shouted. "Don't abuse your power as a soldier by extorting money and falsely accusing helpless people. Be content with your pay, and be thankful you have food and clothing."

He certainly had sized me up correctly. I wondered how. Perhaps it was because so many of my fellow soldiers were guilty of the same crimes. All these things John commanded I wanted to do. I truly did want to rid myself of the guilt and shame that burdened me. But how could I be sure of God's forgiveness? How could I know that John's words were true and those of Mithras false?

As I considered these things, a quiet came over the crowd. Another man was making his way toward John. The tax collector and I had found it necessary to push and elbow our way to the head of line, but this man simply passed through, the people making way without protest, strangely awed by his presence. It was Jesus, the prophet from Galilee, himself coming for baptism.

John seemed puzzled and hesitated. Trying to deter Jesus, he said, "I need to be baptized by you, and do you come to me?" But Jesus insisted, "Let it be so now; it is proper for us to do this, to fulfill all righteousness."

With that, John consented, pouring water over one who surely had no sins to forgive. At that very moment I heard a voice like thunder. It came from no one in the crowd. It was not John's voice. It was just there, making the ground tremble as it spoke. "You are my Son, whom I love; with you I am well pleased," the voice proclaimed of Jesus.

Then, as silently as he had come among the people to the edge of the water, Jesus melted back into the crowd. Who was he? Whose Son was he? Just what would he do to please his Father whose voice I heard? What did the voice mean? These were the questions that troubled my mind as John's hands drenched me with water.

I lingered there with the tax collector till late afternoon, straining to hear every word John spoke, wondering how I would live this repentance to which I had pledged myself. I was truly sorry. I desperately needed forgiveness, but I also knew myself. I was a tough, old soldier with the ingrained habits acquired from many years of camp and barracks and combat. Surely I would fail. What then?

As I pondered this problem, once more Jesus walked by. All eyes turned toward him. Again there was that profound hush. John, his hand on the dripping head of a young man, turned his eyes until they met the penetrating gaze of Jesus. Slowly John lifted his hand from the young man and pointed toward the Galilean.

Distinctly and deliberately John spoke, "Look! The Lamb of God who takes away the sins of the world!"

That was the answer to my question, to my concerns about the certainty of forgiveness for sins past and future. Jesus would take my sins away! Somehow he would be the sacrificial Lamb that would cleanse me. It would be three-and-a-half years before I learned just how he would be that sacrifice. My own governor, my own fellow soldiers with whom I might have bunked in years past would put him to death on a cross. I would be there, watching, and listening, horrified, yet unable to do anything, unsure that I should try, thinking that somehow this was planned.

On that dark day, words I have never forgotten came together in a wholeness that would determine my identity and the direction my life would take. Three-and-a-half years before, I had heard a voice say of Jesus, "This is my Son." Then I had heard John identify Jesus as "the Lamb of God who takes away the sins of the world." Now as I watched Jesus die, I was hearing him pray, "Father, forgive them." In my heart, I knew I was included in that prayer, a prayer that would most certainly be heard. It's still fresh in my mind even today. I went on to finish out my enlistment. I got my pension and farm. I married my common-law wife, the mother of my children. They and I are all officially citizens of Rome, now. But Roman citizen is not my most cherished identity. The identity I cherish most is that of a citizen of the kingdom of God, a citizenship earned in battle, not my battle, but Jesus' battle for me when he died in my place on the cross. Because of him, I am no longer just Miles, retired soldier of Rome with a farm in Galatia, but Miles, forgiven sinner, servant of Jesus with a home in heaven.

Prayer

Lord God, rescue us from rationalizing our sins. Transform us into servants of Jesus who delight in doing good to our neighbor. Help us believe that the forgiveness you granted tax collectors and soldiers is for us, too. Thank you for granting our prayer, for Jesus' sake. Amen.

Good Friday

Worship Bulletin

What Wondrous Love Is This?
(A Tenebrae Service)

(The Service of Tenebrae goes back to the eighth century, and perhaps earlier. "Tenebrae" is Latin for "darkness" or "shadows" and refers to the progressive darkening of the church as candles are put out one by one. The dimming of lights reminds us of Christ dying on the cross, as well as the fading loyalty of the disciples. One candle in our church, the Christ candle, remains burning, though it is carried out and brought back near the end of the service signifying hope in his resurrection. The Strepitus, *the loud sound of a book closing, symbolizes the finished work of Christ, his death, and the closing of the tomb. Though we leave the church in somber reflection on Good Friday, we return on Easter Sunday to a church filled with light and joyful shouts of "Alleluia, Christ is risen!")*

Preparation
Silent Procession Of The Cross
(stand as cross and Christ candle enter at the sound of the bell)

Invocation
P: In the name of the Father and of the Son and of the Holy Spirit.
C: Amen.

Confession And Forgiveness
P: Let us confess our sins to God our Father.
C: Father, I have sinned against heaven and against you. I am no longer worthy to be called your son. God have mercy on me, a sinner. Have mercy on me, O God, according to your unfailing love; according to your great

compassion blot out my transgressions. **Wash away all my iniquity and cleanse me from my sin** (Luke 15:21; Luke 18:13; Psalm 51:1-2).

P: If you confess with your mouth "Jesus is Lord," and believe in your heart that God raised him from the dead, you will be saved. For it is with your heart that you believe and are justified, and it is with your mouth that you confess and are saved (Romans 10:9-10). In the stead and by the command of my Lord Jesus Christ, I, as a called servant of the Word, announce the forgiveness of all your sins in the name of the Father and of the Son and of the Holy Spirit.

All: Amen.

Hymn "In The Cross"

The Word

Introduction John 15:13
Reader 1

Pastor

P: Gracious Lord, your Word says that you are love. Help us see this love in the suffering and death of your Son for sinners. Move us to respond to this love in faith. Grant that the love we receive from you would shine from us in acts of selfless love to others. In the name of Jesus we pray.

All: Amen.

Hymn "Go To Dark Gethsemane"

Part I
The Upper Room —
Wondrous Acts Of Love

Reader 2 John 13:1-5

Pastor

Hymn "What Wondrous Love Is This?" (v. 1)

Part II
The Garden Of Gethsemane —
Wondrous Example Of Love

Reader 1 — Matthew 26:30, 36-46; Luke 22:47-51

Pastor

Reader 2

Pastor

Hymn — "What Wondrous Love Is This?" (v. 2)

Part III
At The Home Of The High Priest —
Wondrous Look Of Love

Reader 1 — Luke 22:54-62

Pastor

Hymn — "What Wondrous Love Is This?" (v. 3)

Part IV
In The Court Of The Governor —
Wondrous Silence Of Love

Reader 2 — Matthew 27:11-14; John 19:1-16

Pastor

Hymn — "What Wondrous Love Is This?" (v. 4)

Part V
At Calvary —
Wondrous Words Of Love

The First Wondrous Word Of Love — Luke 23:34

"Father, forgive them, for they do not know what they are doing."

Pastor

Reader 1

(The first candle is put out. A bell sounds.)

Hymn "O Sacred Head" (v. 1)

The Second Wondrous Word Of Love Luke 23:43
"I tell you the truth, today you will be with me in paradise."

Pastor

Reader 1

(The second candle is put out. A bell sounds.)

Hymn "O Sacred Head" (v. 2)

The Third Wondrous Word Of Love John 19:26-27
"Dear woman, here is your son ... Here is your mother."

Pastor

Reader 1

Pastor

Reader 1

(The third candle is put out. A bell sounds.)

Hymn "O Sacred Head" (v. 3)

The Fourth Wondrous Word Of Love Mark 15:34
"Eloi, Eloi, lama sabachthani? ... My God, my God, why have you forsaken me?"

Pastor

Reader 1

(The fourth candle is put out. A bell sounds.)

Hymn "O Sacred Head" (v. 4)

The Fifth Wondrous Word Of Love John 19:28
"I thirst."

Pastor

Reader 1

(The fifth candle is put out. A bell sounds.)

Hymn "O Sacred Head" (v. 5)

The Sixth Wondrous Word Of Love John 19:30
"It is finished!"

Pastor

Reader 1

(The sixth candle is put out. A bell rings six times.)

Hymn "O Sacred Head" (v. 6)

The Seventh Wondrous Word Of Love Luke 23:46
"Father, into your hands I commit my spirit."

Pastor

Reader 1

(All lights are dimmed. The Christ candle is carried out and returned, signifying the death of Christ but holding forth the promise of resurrection. The Strepitus *— the slamming of the book — sounds, recalling the closing of the tomb.)*

Hymn "Were You There?" (vv. 1-4)

Part VI

Conclusion
Pastor

Hymn "Jesus Remember Me"
(or another song or a moment of silence)

Lord's Prayer
Our Father who art in heaven, hallowed be thy name, thy kingdom come, thy will be done on earth as it is in heaven.

Give us this day our daily bread; and forgive us our trespasses as we forgive those who trespass against us; and lead us not into temptation, but deliver us from evil.

For thine is the kingdom and the power and the glory forever and ever. Amen.

Silent Prayer

Silent Recession Of The Cross
(Stand and face the cross as it exits. Leave in silence.)

(While no offering is taken during the service, gifts may be placed at the door when exiting.)

Good Friday

Scripture And Readings

What Wondrous Love Is This?

The Word
Introduction
Reader 1: Greater love has no one than this, that he lay down his life for his friends (John 15:13).

Pastor: Love — at one and the same time it is perhaps the most meaningless and meaningful word in our language. It's what we sing about in our popular songs. It's the standard fare of the silver screen. It's what enraptured lovers pledge to each other when the fires of romance burn brightly, but what they often forget when troubles come. It is perhaps our highest ideal, but such an elusive one! As someone has said, "I love my fellow man. It's people I can't stand."

We want to love. We want to be loved. We know what is when we experience it. But just what is it? The New Testament meaning of love is found in the word *agape*, a word that is perhaps as old as the Greek language, but seldom used in ancient literature by anyone but Christians. *Agape* is love without regard for the worthiness of the one who is loved. It is love that sacrifices oneself for the benefit of another. It is love that finds its origin in God. It is wondrous. It is what we see in Jesus.

Tonight we consider the wondrous love of Jesus as heard in his words and seen in his actions during the events of Maundy Thursday and Good Friday of the first Holy Week. We begin in the upper room where Jesus celebrates the Last Supper with his disciples. But first, let us pray before we begin our journey to the cross.

Gracious Lord, your word says that you are love. Help us to see this love in the suffering and death of your Son for sinners. Move us to respond to this love in faith. Grant that the love we receive from you would shine from us in acts of selfless love to others. In the name of Jesus we pray.

Congregation: Amen.

Part I
The Upper Room —
Wondrous Acts Of Love

Reader 2: It was just before the Passover Feast. Jesus knew that the time had come for him to leave this world and go to the Father. Having loved his own who were in the world, he now showed them the full extent of his love. The evening meal was being served, and the devil had already prompted Judas Iscariot, son of Simon, to betray Jesus. Jesus knew that the Father had put all things under his power, and that he had come from God and was returning to God; so he got up from the meal, took off his outer clothing, and wrapped a towel around his waist. After that, he poured water into a basin and began to wash his disciples' feet, drying them with the towel that was wrapped around him (John 13:1-5).

Pastor: Streets generally weren't paved in Bible times and people wore sandals. Often the city sewer was simply a ditch in the middle of the road. Garbage was thrown out doors and windows. Manure from cattle and donkeys lay where it fell. Add to this the dust kicked up by dozens of animals and people, and one's feet would be filthy by the time a pedestrian reached his destination. So custom dictated that the host provide his guests with a basin and towel that they might wash their feet, or if the host were wealthy, his slave would do it.

But at the Last Supper, something most unusual happened. The host, Jesus, took the role of the slave and washed the disciples' feet for them. It had to be done, yet none of them had volunteered to do it. So Jesus did, and in so doing demonstrated the character of his kingdom. It would be a kingdom of slaves who served not because they had to but because they wanted to. The ones they served would not be just their blood relatives, not just brothers and sisters in the faith, not just a favorite neighbor, but even their enemies.

This was a radically different concept of love. As the evening in the upper room wore on, the events that unfolded showed just how radically different Jesus' understanding of love was. Judas had already betrayed Jesus. He held in his purse that very night the silver coins he had earned as the price of his betrayal. Yet Jesus, in love, ate that holy meal with him, and then, before Judas left, our Lord gently washed his feet. This is love that defies definition. It is love that raises the mark. This is love great enough to include you and me. What wondrous love is this?

Hymn   "What Wondrous Love Is This?" (v. 1)

Part II
The Garden Of Gethsemane —
Wondrous Example Of Love

Reader 1: When they had sung a hymn, they went out to the Mount of Olives.

Then Jesus went with his disciples to a place called Gethsemane, and said to them, "Sit here while I go over there and pray." He took Peter and the two sons of Zebedee along with him, and he began to be sorrowful and troubled. Then he said to them, "My soul is overwhelmed with sorrow to the point of death. Stay here and keep watch with me."

Going a little farther, he fell with his face to the ground and prayed, "My Father, if it is possible, may this cup be taken from me. Yet not as I will, but as you will."

Then he returned to his disciples and found them sleeping. "Could you men not keep watch with me for one hour?" he asked Peter. "Watch and pray so that you will not fall into temptation. The spirit is willing, but the body is weak."

He went away a second time and prayed, "My Father, if it is not possible for this cup to be taken away unless I drink it, may your will be done." When he came back, he again found them sleeping, because their eyes were heavy. So he left them and went away once more and prayed the third time, saying the same thing.

Then he returned to the disciples and said to them, "Are you still sleeping and resting? Look, the hour is near, and the Son of Man is betrayed into the hands of sinners. Rise, let us go! Here comes my betrayer" (Matthew 26:30, 36-46).

Pastor: As Jesus prays in Gethsemane, we learn another aspect of his wondrous love. It is love that resolves to act on behalf of another even when the contemplated act of love is repugnant to the one who does the loving. It is love that resolves to act when the object of that love is manifestly unworthy. Such love is almost inconceivable to us. We can perhaps imagine ourselves caring for a relative through a grave and unpleasant illness, assisting with the necessary tasks of feeding, of washing, or changing the dressing on a wound. A mother willingly does such things for her child, or a husband for his wife. But seldom would we do that for one we are unrelated to. And if we do, surely we would expect and even demand payment, as would a nurse or nurse's assistant.

The task was no more pleasant for Jesus than it would have been for us. In Gethsemane, Jesus envisions the nauseating and excruciating agony that lies ahead, the price he must pay to heal our sin-sick souls, and he pleads with God to relieve him of the awful responsibility. Three times Jesus begs God to take away the cup, but three times he also prays, "Your will be done." Dying on the cross in itself is horrifying, but doing so to save others who are clearly so undeserving, is simply unthinkable. Yet that is exactly what Jesus has determined to do.

Jesus is about to be arrested by a mob out for blood. He asks his disciples to keep watch as he prays. He prays for them, for you and me, for himself. And they fall asleep! Again and again, they fall asleep as though his suffering means nothing to them! And yet, in his prayer, he recommits himself to the task for which he came, the task of giving up his life for sinners who can't even keep watch for one hour! He goes to the cross, securing by the blood of his tortured body eternal life for you and me, and we can't even give him sixty minutes of our undivided attention! What wondrous love is this?

Reader 2: While he was still speaking a crowd came up, and the man who was called Judas, one of the twelve, was leading them. He approached Jesus to kiss him, but Jesus asked him, "Judas, are you betraying the Son of Man with a kiss?"

When Jesus' followers saw what was going to happen, they said, "Lord, should we strike with our swords?" And one of them struck the servant of the high priest, cutting off his right ear.

But Jesus answered, "No more of this!" And he touched the man's ear and healed him (Luke 22:47-51).

Pastor: How would you react at the sight of a mob carrying torches and weapons seeking to lynch you in the middle of the night? I think I'd run. I'd die from exhaustion before they could catch me. We know from his prayer that Jesus would like to have done the same thing, but nothing would deter him from doing what he came to do, giving his life as a ransom for sinners. That inner battle had been won when Jesus prayed that last time, "Not my will but yours be done."

But Jesus is not just a passive victim, or shall we say passive lover of sinners, in this scene of the passion drama. Not only does he allow himself to be arrested, but he intervenes on behalf of the very mob that has come to kill him. When his disciples chafe to draw their swords in defense of their Master, and Peter actually does so, slicing off the ear of the nearest enemy, Jesus tells him to put the sword back. "No more of this!" he says. Then he tenderly picks up the severed ear of Malchus, the slave of Caiaphas, and heals him. Malchus comes as an enemy. Jesus meets him as a friend and healer. That's redemptive love. That's wondrous love.

Hymn   "What Wondrous Love Is This?" (v. 2)

Part III
At The Home Of The High Priest —
Wondrous Look Of Love

Reader 1: Then seizing him, they led him away and took him into the house of the high priest. Peter followed at a distance. But when they had kindled a fire in the middle of the courtyard and had sat down together, Peter sat down with them. A servant girl saw him seated there in the firelight. She looked closely at him and said, "This man was with him."

But he denied it. "Woman, I don't know him," he said.

A little later someone else saw him and said, "You are also one of them."

"Man, I am not!" Peter replied.

About an hour later another asserted, "Certainly this fellow was with him, for he is a Galilean."

Peter replied, "Man, I don't know what you are talking about!" Just as he was speaking, the rooster crowed. The Lord turned and looked straight at Peter. Then Peter remembered the word the Lord had spoken to him: "Before the rooster crows today, you will disown me three times." And he went outside and wept bitterly (Luke 22:54-62).

Pastor: "If looks could kill!" we've sometimes said, describing the gleam of daggers coming from angry eyes. Is that what Peter felt when Jesus looked at him as the cock crowed? "Even if all fall away on account of you, I never will," Peter had boasted only hours before. But Jesus knew better. "This very night before the rooster crows, you will disown me three times," he had replied. Surely Peter's intentions were good. Surely he meant his words when he spoke them. I'm sure he also planned to stay awake when Jesus asked him to keep watch while he prayed. "The spirit is willing but the flesh is weak," Jesus had said of his sleeping disciples. That seems to apply to all our good intentions.

Peter intended good, but he lacked the ability to do the good he intended, as do we all. How many of us have made promises and vows before God at our baptism or the baptism of our children, at our wedding, at our confirmation? We would rather suffer death than fall away from Christ and his church, we have pledged. "Till death do us part," we've promised our partner, only to divorce a few years later. There's a little of Simon Peter in all of us.

If the cock crowed every time we had denied Jesus three times in row, how often would we hear it in a day? I suspect before the day was done, the rooster would be in the doctor's office suffering from a sore throat. But back to that look Jesus gave Peter. Was it the glint of daggers that Peter felt, the pain of God's wrath penetrating his body like honed steel? I don't think so. That would be so out of character for Jesus. Far from wrath, I think the look Jesus gave Peter was one of pity and grace. "You've done exactly as I predicted, Peter," Jesus seems to be saying with that look. "You've denied me three times in your weakness and fallen condition as a sinner. Yet that is why I am standing here now, being falsely accused, humiliated, tortured. I'm here to have the wrath of God that your sins deserve directed at me. Mine is not the look of anger Peter, or hatred, but of love."

I think Peter recognized that look of love when the eyes of Jesus turned toward him. It brought Peter to his senses. "I've denied my best friend and yet he still loves me!" Peter must be saying in his heart. These tears that he sheds are not the tears of one who has been flogged, but one who realizes he is loved, in spite of his unworthiness. These are the tears of a saved sinner, grieving at what he has done, rejoicing to know that he is loved and forgiven. No, it wasn't anger in that look Jesus gave Peter, but a look of mercy and love, wondrous love.

Hymn "What Wondrous Love Is This?" (v. 3)

Part IV
In The Court Of The Governor —
Wondrous Silence Of Love

Reader 2: Meanwhile Jesus stood before the governor, and the governor asked him, "Are you the king of the Jews?"

"Yes, it is as you say," Jesus replied.

When he was accused by the chief priests and the elders, he gave no answer. Then Pilate asked him, "Don't you hear the testimony they are bringing against you?" But Jesus made no reply, not even to a single charge — to the great amazement of the governor (Matthew 27:11-14).

Then Pilate took Jesus and had him flogged. The soldiers twisted together a crown of thorns and put it on his head. They clothed him in a purple robe and went up to him again and again, saying, "Hail, king of the Jews!" And they struck him in the face.

Once more Pilate came out and said to the Jews, "Look, I am bringing him out to you to let you know that I find no basis for a charge against him. When Jesus came out wearing the crown of thorns and the purple robe, Pilate said to them, 'Here is the man!' "

As soon as the chief priests and their officials saw him, they shouted, "Crucify! Crucify!" But Pilate answered, "You take him and crucify him. As for me, I find no basis for a charge against him."

The Jews insisted, "We have a law, and according to that law, he must die, because he claimed to be the Son of God."

When Pilate heard this, he was even more afraid, and he went back inside the palace. "Where do you come from?" he asked Jesus, but Jesus gave him no answer. "Do you refuse to speak to me?" Pilate said, "Don't you realize I have power to either free you or to crucify you?"

Jesus answered, "You would have no power over me if it were not given to you from above. Therefore the one who handed me over to you is guilty of a greater sin."

From then on, Pilate tried to set Jesus free, but the Jews kept shouting, "If you let this man go, you are no friend of Caesar. Anyone who claims to be a king opposes Caesar."

When Pilate heard this, he brought Jesus out and sat down on the judge's seat known as the stone pavement (which in Aramaic is *Gabbatha*). It was the day of Preparation of Passover Week, about the sixth hour.

"Here is your king," Pilate said to the Jews.

But they shouted, "Take him away! Take him away!"

"Shall I crucify your king?" Pilate asked.

"We have no king but Caesar," the chief priests answered.

Finally Pilate handed him over to them to be crucified (John 19:1-16).

Pastor: An innocent man is falsely accused. If convicted, he faces the death penalty, and yet he says nothing in his own defense! This is unthinkable, yet that is exactly what happened at the several trials of Jesus. I say several trials because that is what Jesus was subjected to during the pre-dawn hours of Good Friday; first a trial before the high priest, then a trial before Pilate, then one before Herod Tetrarch of Galilee, then again before Pilate.

Oh, Jesus did say a few things, curiously obscure things, when questioned. "Are you the king of the Jews?" Pilate asks him. "Is that your own idea or did others talk to you about me?" Jesus answers. Jesus doesn't tell Pilate who he is. It's up to Pilate to make that decision. Earlier at the high priest's house, Jesus is asked, "Are you the Christ, the Son of God?" To which Jesus cryptically replies, "You have said."

Why doesn't Jesus just give a straight answer? Because the only answer that matters is the one that comes by faith from the heart. All the evidence anyone needs is there in the gospels. There we see his acts of mercy; healing the sick, giving sight to the blind, cleansing lepers, making the crippled walk, forgiving tax collectors and prostitutes. Then we are asked to decide for ourselves who Jesus is. It makes no difference who someone else says he is. For our lives to change, we are asked to make our own confession of who Jesus is. So Jesus teaches. He acts. He leaves us with the decision, just as he did Pilate.

What a weak-willed man Pilate seems to be! He does everything he can to be rid of this problem of what to do about Jesus. He tries to release him. He tries to hand him off to Herod of Galilee. He tries to get Jesus to say something in his own defense. He tells the crowd there's no evidence of a capital offense. He pleads with Jesus to work with him, if only a little, but Jesus says nothing.

Pilate is in a predicament. His conscience tells him Jesus is an innocent man who deserves to go free. But his practical nature as a politician tells him that if he frees Jesus, the crowd will see to it that he loses his job. What a weasel, yet Jesus even has compassion for him. Jesus knows Pilate is being forced to bend to the crowd's demands. But rather than shame the governor for his cowardice, there is a note of grace in the few words that Jesus finally speaks, "The one who handed me over to you is guilty of a greater sin."

What kind of man would break his silence to speak words of grace to the very judge condemning him to death? A man of uncommon love, wondrous love, that's who.

Hymn "What Wondrous Love Is This?" (v. 4)

Part V
At Calvary —
Wondrous Words Of Love

The First Wondrous Word Of Love

Pastor: The suffering of Jesus proceeds rapidly to its conclusion after Pilate's decision. Jesus, with Pilate's permission, is flogged. Stripped of his clothing, the soldiers throw a purple military cape over his bleeding back. Pressing a crown of thorns into his scalp and placing a reed in his right hand for a mace, they pretend to worship him. Kneeling, they mock Jesus saying, "Hail, king of the Jews." Laughing, they spit on him, strike him in the face, and when they're finished with their fun, after Pilate has finally agreed to the death sentence, they lead Jesus out, carrying his own cross to be crucified.

At Golgotha, also known as, "Calvary, the Place of the Skull," the soldiers offer Jesus a drugged beverage to help him bear the pain. He refuses it. At about 9:00 a.m. Friday morning, Jesus is crucified. Nails are pounded through his wrists and ankles into the wood of the cross which is then hoisted up and dropped into a hole cut for it in the rock. A sign is fastened above his head, stating the charge against him written by Pilate. It reads, "This is Jesus of Nazareth, the King of the Jews." As the soldiers gamble for his clothes, Jesus speaks his first words from the cross, wondrous words, words of love.

Reader 1: "Father, forgive them, for they do not know what they are doing" (Luke 23:34).

(The first candle is put out. A bell sounds.)

Hymn "O Sacred Head" (v. 1)

The Second Wondrous Word Of Love
Pastor: The mockery that began in the trials of Jesus continues from all quarters at the cross. "You who would destroy the temple and build it in three days, save yourself," passersby deride him. If Jesus were motivated by anything but love for these very people, he would save himself. But *agape* love says, "No," to self, and "Yes," to the needs of others. So for now, Jesus listens in pained silence. As if mocking another would somehow bring dignity to themselves, the criminals condemned to die with Jesus add their own insults to the din. "Are you not the Christ?" they shout. "Save yourself and us!" Perhaps their words are part derision and partly cries of despair. But Jesus does not answer. He agonizes alone.

As the morning grows late, one criminal has a change of heart. Jesus is different from all other lawbreakers and condemned men he has seen in his life of crime. Jesus is reviled mercilessly, but when he speaks, they are words of mercy. This lone criminal, the first voice of faith raised since Gethsemane, cries out in rebuke of his partner in crime. "Do you not fear God since we are under the same condemnation? And we indeed justly, for we are getting what we deserve for what we have done; but this man has done nothing wrong." Then he turns to Jesus and pleads for grace, "Jesus, remember me when you come into your kingdom." Again, as we have come to expect, words of wondrous love are spoken by the Savior.

Reader 1: "I tell you the truth, today you will be with me in paradise" (Luke 23:43).

(The second candle is put out. A bell sounds.)

Hymn "O Sacred Head" (v. 2)

The Third Wondrous Word Of Love
Pastor: Not all near the cross are enemies of Jesus delighting to taunt and torture him. Some are friends and relatives whose hearts are breaking but who can do nothing for the one they love and the

one who loves them. One is Mary, Jesus' mother, now a widow and soon to need care in her old age. She, doubtless, has not even thought of the desperate situation that confronts her. Her mind is filled only with the suffering of her son and her inability to help him. But Jesus, dying, his body wracked with pain, thinks of her needs and not his own, and speaks words of wondrous love. To his beloved mother he says,

Reader 1: "Dear woman, here is your son ..." (John 19:26b).

Pastor: And to the disciple who stood near her, the disciple he loved most dearly, he says,

Reader 1: "Here is your mother" (John 19:27a).

(The third candle is put out. A bell sounds.)

Hymn "O Sacred Head" (v. 3)

The Fourth Wondrous Word Of Love
Pastor: At about noon on Good Friday, a strange darkness covers the whole land. We can imagine that this had an immediately sobering effect on the noisy crowd that so far looked on this whole affair as something of a lark in the park. It doesn't normally get dark at noon unless there's an eclipse. And even if it were an eclipse that obscured the light of the sun, it would be interpreted in those days as an omen, and not a good one. Things would have gotten very quiet about now. Only a few kept up their jeering. Others would be having second thoughts.

In the darkness and growing quiet Jesus cries out again, wondrous words that only reveal their content of love with serious reflection. The holy Son of God is now laden with the entire sin and guilt of mankind, your sin and mine. God the Father turns away from his own Son who has become sin for us. Jesus, in the space of a few hours, endures an eternity of God's wrath that we sinners deserve. What incomprehensible words of wondrous love for you and me are contained in this despairing cry of Jesus,

Reader 1: *"Eloi, Eloi, lama sabachthani?* ... My God, my God, why have you forsaken me?" (Mark 15:34).

(The fourth candle is put out. A bell sounds.)

Hymn "O Sacred Head" (v. 4)

The Fifth Wondrous Word Of Love

Pastor: The end is not far off now. Jesus has not eaten or had anything to drink since the Last Supper with his disciples that now seems ages ago. He is physically drained from fatigue, from loss of blood, from hunger, and from dehydration. Having endured everything, including separation from his Father, Jesus the divine Son of God, at last expresses a personal need, and in doing so once more identifies with mortal human beings in their frailty. What wondrous love is this that moved the Incarnate Word to share our flesh, humbling himself to experience our needs, including the need for something to drink?

Reader 1: "I thirst" (John 19:28).

(The fifth candle is put out. A bell sounds.)

Hymn "O Sacred Head" (v. 5)

The Sixth Wondrous Word Of Love

Pastor: At about three o'clock, the promise of the ages has been fulfilled. The Savior has completed the work his Father sent him to do. The sins of the world have been atoned for. God is no longer alienated from mankind. He is reconciled to us all. The arms of his Son, still nailed to the cross beam, are opened wide beckoning every prodigal child of God to return home and share in the love and forgiveness purchased at great cost by Jesus. We pause and wonder at these loving words of Jesus that no religious effort of man, no good work, no act of penance can ever improve on.

Reader 1: "It is finished!" (John 19:30).

(The sixth candle is put out. A bell rings six times.)

Hymn "O Sacred Head" (v. 6)

The Seventh Wondrous Word Of Love
Pastor: Now, many hours after the ordeal began, Jesus is about to die. He takes his last labored breath, he is released from all his agony, all his humiliation, all the injustice he endured for you and me. The earth begins to rumble with an earthquake as Jesus, with what seems like the shout of a victorious warrior, cries out to his Father one last prayer.

Reader 1: "Father, into your hands I commit my spirit" (Luke 23:46).

(All lights are dimmed. The Christ candle is carried out and returned, signifying the death of Christ but holding forth the promise of resurrection. The Strepitus *— the slamming of the book — sounds, recalling the closing of the tomb.)*

Hymn "Were You There?" (vv. 1-4)

Part VI
Conclusion
Pastor: It's all over now, all but the burial, all but the lonely weeping of a handful of friends and Jesus' mother, all but the waiting until Sunday morning when the Sabbath is over and we can visit the tomb. But we don't despair. One last candle still flickers, signaling our hope that the death of Jesus is not the end. So we leave expectantly, certain that though the tomb is closed now, in just three short days it will open, revealing that our Lord lives, never to die again. And, because he lives, we shall live also. What wondrous love is this!

Hymn "Jesus, Remember Me" (vv. 1-4)
(or another song, or a moment of silence)

The Lord's Prayer

Silent Prayer

Silent Recession Of The Cross
(Stand and face the cross as it exits. Leave in silence.)